To Jimmy,
I hope that you
enjoy the Stars
of News Gyt MSgers!
All the best,
Bob Morris Cella

FIXING THE MOON

The Story of The First Presidential Pilot And Aviation Pioneer
Lt. Col. Henry Tift Myers

Bonne Davis Cella

Henchard Press, Ltd.

Publisher	Henry S. Beers
Associate Publisher	Richard J. Hutto
Executive Vice President	Robert G. Aldrich
Operations Manager	Gary G. Pulliam
Editor-in-Chief	Joni Woolf
Art Director/Designer	Julianne Gleaton
Director of Marketing and Media Relations	Mary D. Robinson

Printed in India

Library of Congress Control Number: 2005934674

ISBN: (10 digit) 0-9770912-0-1
(13 digit) 978-0-9770912-0-1

 Henchard Press, Ltd.

Henchard Press, Ltd. books are available at quantity discounts
with bulk purchase for educational, business, or sales promotional use.
For information, please write to:
Henchard Press, Ltd., 3920 Ridge Avenue, Macon, GA 31210, or call 866-311-9578.
www.henchardpress.com

Table Of Contents

Acknowledgements...**5**

Preface **6**

Introduction...**8**

Chapter One **10**
Preparing For Take Off

Chapter Two..**42**
Cruising Altitude

Chapter Three..**104**
Final Approach

Epilogue **158**
Smooth Landings

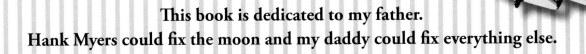

This book is dedicated to my father.
Hank Myers could fix the moon and my daddy could fix everything else.

Claude Montgomery Davis
July 31, 1928-September 9, 2002

Georgia Military College 1945

Acknowledgements

Thank you, my sons, Tony and Chris, for your encouragement, suggestions, and patience as I trudged through the writing process. Mother, credit goes to you for showing me examples of fortitude, determination, and perseverance in all of your life endeavors. Little brother Davy, thank you for lovingly writing and recording the ballad "Fixing the Moon"—it has added much joy to this project. Patti Stafford, I thank you, sweet friend, for proofing my manuscript the first time and offering your skilled writing suggestions. Appreciation goes to you, Liz Carson Keith, Tommy Rankin, and Frank Masland for sharing cherished family photographs. Kay Baldwin, I thank you for sending the scrapbook you meticulously kept through the years on your good friend, Hank Myers. Clark Skillman, thank you for taking me to the American Airlines Archives and making copies of photographs. Dr. and Mrs. Dennis Plunk of Dumas, Texas, you have my deepest appreciation and gratitude. For after learning that you had purchased from a military dealer, pictures, letters, and other memorabilia once belonging to Hank Myers, I, a total stranger, called you to ask if I might make copies of the pictures of Hank to include in this book. Within a few short days, fifty-one pounds of material relating to Hank arrived at my home, donated by you to help us start a permanent display for Hank Myers. Thank you both so much for your generosity. Sherry Gatewood and Jo Wingate, my prayer warrior friends, you have lifted me up so many times and I love you. Margie Coleman, your kind note containing a stick of chewing gum and the words Stick To It brought me back to the project many times and I appreciate your support. And finally to you, dear Tift, thank you for trusting me and for sharing so much of yourself and your family—I hope that you are pleased with the book and I hope that you enjoyed this journey as much as I did.

Preface

There must be a quirky gene that runs in my family because most of us like to dig. Given the opportunity, we churn in the soil and clay for hours on end looking for arrowheads, Civil War mini-balls, old coins, "turn-of- the-century" bottles, and Indian pottery pieces. While at the beach, rather than relaxing, we dig in the sand looking for worn and weathered "beach glass" or ancient shark teeth. It seems that we have an addiction to and fascination with unearthing remnants of days gone by.

When I was allowed to survey the material relating to the life of Lt. Col. Henry Tift Myers, it was like finding the mother lode, and, I did not have to worry about rattlesnakes, gnats, or sunburn. In a comfortable setting with my reading glasses at hand, I began my exploration. The boxes were literally overflowing with history—black and white photographs of exotic locations and beautiful people with famous faces. It soon became a ritual on Saturday nights—the boxes and me. I was imbued with feelings of romance, adventure, and curiosity that seemed to seep out of the worn and tattered boxes. Hiding under the dust and folds of time were original letters and documents from famous leaders of World War II. Also scattered around were pictures, letters, and logbooks that documented historic events as they unfolded. The more I found, the more convinced I became that the life and career of Henry Tift (Hank) Myers should be recorded in a book and shared with others.

Hank Myers was approached several times during his life with various book proposals but always declined. Although he was a brazen and courageous pilot, he was sometimes quite timid and not one to self-promote. Maybe though, in some other dimension, he changed his mind about sharing his extraordinary life. Once opened, the boxes of his memories captivated this writer and the coincidences that followed were signposts that it was time to tell Hank's story. It was, after all, the one-hundredth anniversary of flight. Perhaps in honor of the anniversary, Hank Myers' spirit willed for this story to be told. It would be a story about a dashing pilot who flew presidents and kings and charted new routes while setting world records for speed and distance. It would also be a story about a man who romanced beautiful women all over the globe and indulged his leisure pursuits. And finally, it would be a story about the pilot's only child, Tift, the son who lost his way in life but was able to find peace and liberation by returning to his father's roots. There in the small South Georgia town where Hank's story began, Tift would return to gain a deep appreciation for his family legacy and a renewed respect for his father—the father who could fix the moon!

Introduction

In the summer of 1968, Tift Myers was invited to drive with his father the 1200 miles from Fort Worth, Texas, to Sea Island, Georgia. Hank Myers had been giving serious thought to moving back to Georgia and wanted Tift to come along with him to look at coastal real estate. Tift eagerly said yes because he thought that the long ride would give them time to talk and hopefully establish a closer relationship. In years past, they had been separated by divorce and a career. When Tift did get to see his father, it was never just the two of them; there was always a lovely woman around vying for Hank Myers' attention.

Among the many hobbies and passions that Hank Myers enjoyed was automobiles. For this trip they would ride in his new yellow Buick Rivera GS with two four-barrel carburetors. Equipped with a "fuzz buster," they would make the drive in record time. Hank Myers was used to setting world records in the air, so why not on the road as well? Tift also loved cars and speed and much of their conversation during the trip revolved around that subject.

They arrived in Tifton for a "pit stop" and for a visit with family and friends. Pearl Myers, Hank's mother, had died three years earlier but Marguerite, his sister, and Doll, a long time friend and employee of the family, could not have been happier to see them. The ladies had been busy baking in anticipation of their visit. Marguerite's signature daisy-shaped cheese biscuits were neatly packed in tins for snacking and there were plenty extra for them to take along to Sea Island. Hank and Tift managed to get in a little fishing and the next morning they headed east for the coast.

The Sea Island property was beautiful and, yes, the marina could accommodate Hank's prized boat. A plan was in motion and when Hank returned to Fort Worth, he would do the necessary tying up of loose ends in preparation for the move east.

Hank suggested that for the return trip to Texas they by-pass Tifton and go on up to Atlanta for a couple of nights. Handing Tift some cash and his Playboy Club card, Hank told his son: "Here, go on out and enjoy yourself." Tift looked up a Delta flight attendant that had been a friend from Fort Worth and, yes, she was in town and free for the weekend. She was more than happy to go out and help Tift "do the town." Hank chose a slower, more relaxed venue—Flowery Branch, Ga. Just northeast of Atlanta and right at Lake Lanier, Hank stayed with his favorite cousin, Tom Daniel, where they fished and recalled old times.

It was a wonderful trip that Tift would always remember. Unfortunately, times like these would be no more. Hank Myers died a few months later at the age of sixty-one. He had been retired as a captain for American Airlines for only one year. At some point on their journey, obviously downhearted, Hank quoted these words to Tift: "Clip the wings of a robin and it becomes tame; clip the wings of an eagle and it dies." This highflying eagle of a pilot had been grounded because of his heart condition and he must have known that his days were numbered.

Because of Hank's vantage point in an incredible time in history, Tift is often asked this question: "What sort of man was your father?" Starting at the very beginning, I will attempt to help Tift answer the question by presenting the people and events that molded and shaped his father's life. You are invited to come along as we tell the story of a small-town Georgia boy who seized extraordinary opportunity, coupled it with courage and determination, and actually lived his dreams.

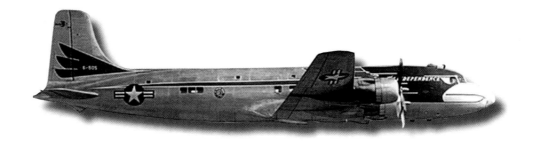

PREPARING FOR TAKE-OFF

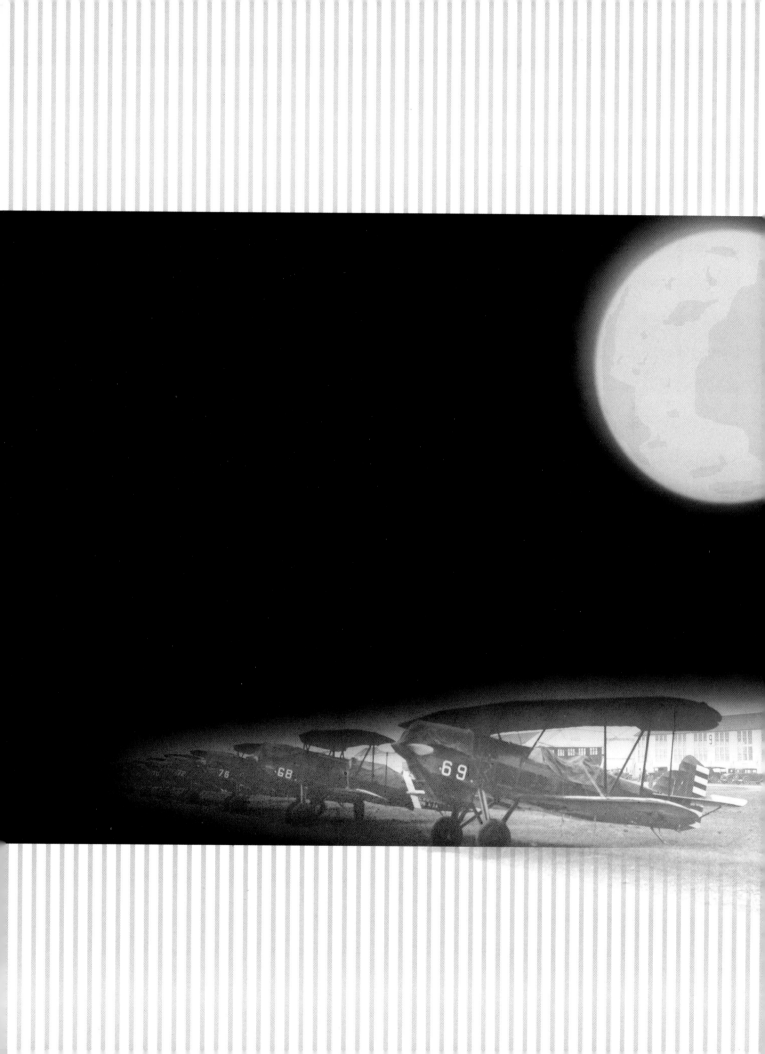

Some people are born when the moon and the stars are so favorably aligned that they soar through life as if it were a vacation planned by a seasoned travel agent. Henry Tift Myers, the first presidential pilot, was born under such conditions to emotionally strong and healthy parents who lived life with purpose and zest. An atmosphere of love and respect resonated from their household and Saint Luke's 12:48 *for unto whomsoever much is given, of him shall be much required* was an understood and accepted way of life.

From this solid foundation, Henry would develop the mettle and confidence to fly presidents, first ladies, senators, congressmen, generals, kings, and thousands of airline passengers. Common sense and humility were his traveling companions—most of the time. He seemed to be unimpressed with his historic aviation records or his unique proximity to power and fame. Flying was part of Henry's being; it was his first love and consumed his interest and imagination. While he was on the ground though, it would be beautiful women, speedboats, and fast cars that would compete for his time and attention.

Henry's father, Irvine Walker Myers, was one of nine sons and his mother, Pearl Willingham Myers, was the youngest of seventeen children. They were considered prosperous business owners and developers in the town of Tifton, Georgia, founded in 1872 by Capt. Henry

Harding Tift. Pearl's older sister, Bessie, had married Captain Tift, making him the uncle and namesake of the future aviator, Henry Tift Myers.

Tifton can be found on the Georgia map at 31° 28'N latitude and 83°31'W longitude. This geographic advantage offers Tifton residents easy access to the bustling capital city of Atlanta or the more tranquil Atlantic coastline. The land is beautiful, the climate is mild, and the people are warm. From antediluvian times, the Lower Creek Indians gently tended the soil and carefully partook of the resources. It was the lure of the abundant and valuable yellow pine forests that first brought the "pale face" settlers to the area. Reading from the introduction to the book, *The History of Tift County* (published in 1948), Lillian Britt Heinsohn beautifully explained the attraction to the region:

To much of the rest of the country, southwest Georgia seemed remote, isolated, sparsely inhabited, and perhaps a little forbidding. But, there was romance and much natural beauty in these pinelands. Throbbing with wild life, redolent with pungent aroma of turpentine, lovely beyond description in its green gothic pine temples. A continuous concert of birds by day; the ecstatic trill of the mockingbird filling the brooding silences of night; the wild fragrance of that night enticing from their hiding places shapes that

Top left, Irvine Walker Myers, one of nine sons.

Tifton

Capt. Henry Harding Tift- The founder of Tifton

Sandbagger Sloop "Annie" Built in 1880 for Captain Tift. Drawing by Russ Humphrey

were silent, elusive, often beautiful. A great silver stag moving with incomparable grace through the moonlight like some disembodied spirit. Little elfin noises in the bushes and brambles, pinecones falling, twigs from gnarled old limbs shattering the silence with their sharp, impatient voices as they break and fall. To witness sundown and "fust-dark" streaming through the majestic trunks of great yellow pines in a blaze of glory was to see a veritable conflagration, a suffusion of molten gold, followed at last by paling, amethystine light and profound silence. These were the things the early settlers knew and loved; and the calm, the tranquility entered into their being and became a part of them and fortified them in their isolation.

By the 1880s, though, Tifton was anything but calm and tranquil—it was more like the Wild West. Men fought for fun and carried their pistols everywhere they went—even to church. One old timer recalled that there were only a few Saturday nights in Tifton when a man was not killed. It was said that men could actually be recognized by the sound of their gunfire. On Saturdays, the turpentine workers would gang up, often becoming dangerous, as they made their way to town looking for adventure. Females would scatter like buckshot when the gang approached, knowing they would have to postpone their shopping and visiting for another time. They scurried back to the safety of their homes as fast as their legs, constrained in long skirts and petticoats, could travel.

Before coming to Georgia and this still remote and unsettled part of the state, Capt. Henry Harding Tift of Mystic, Connecticut, spent most of his time on the high seas. He raced sailing ships and was a marine engineer on ship lines in New York and other coastal ports. Captain Tift's uncle, Nelson Tift, had moved to Georgia in the 1830s, and was the founder of Albany, Georgia (about 42 miles west of Tifton). Nelson operated a manufacturing business there and was in need of an expert engineer. He was able to persuade his nephew to move down from Connecticut and work with him. This proved to be a beneficial and agreeable arrangement for both men. In time, Captain Tift would purchase more than 55,000 acres of pine forest from his uncle in what

15

is now Tift County. With so much virgin timber available, Captain Tift was ready to build his lumber mills and acquired the needed machinery for his mills from a wealthy "transplanted" South Carolinian named Thomas Willingham. Not only would he mill the lumber, Captain Tift would also promote order and help to grow a pleasant little town in this rough and tumble part of the state.

Thomas Willingham and his large family lived between a plantation in Baconton, Georgia, and a home in Radium Springs, Georgia, located near Albany. Leaving behind their beautiful plantation home in Allentown, South Carolina, the Willinghams had moved to escape the ravages of the Civil War.

Born in 1825 at Lawtonville, South Carolina, Thomas Willingham attended Colgate University in Hamilton, New York. He was married to Cecilia Matilda Baynard of Beaufort, South Carolina, who received her education from the Charleston boarding school of Mademoiselle Bonne. Quoting again from *The History of Tift County:*

> To Thomas and Cecilia Baynard Willingham were born seventeen children. Fourteen grew to maturity and all of these attended private schools and college. Most of them were graduated from college and many of them with highest honor.

While attending church on an Easter Sunday morning in Albany, Georgia, the quiet and dignified Captain Tift first saw Bessie, the lovely ninth Willingham child. He knew immediately that she would be his wife, although he was twenty years her senior. At Captain Tift's request, Nelson Tift soon arranged for a proper introduction for his nephew and the young Bessie. Invitations to a party on St. Simons Island were sent and friends and family traveled the one hundred-fifty miles comfortably on board the Brunswick and Albany Railroad. It was on Georgia's romantic St. Simon's Island that Bessie fell in love with the wealthy Captain Tift, and much to her delight when they decided to marry the jeweler sent a large tray

Thomas H. Willingham and his wife Cecilia Baynard Willingham

Pearl Willingham, the youngest of seventeen children

Bessie Willingham, wife of Capt. Henry Harding Tift

of diamonds over to her so that she could make her selection. They married in June of 1885 and spent their early years between Captain Tift's home in Connecticut and their new home in Tifton, named in Captain Tift's honor. Their Tifton home, built in 1872, is known as the Tift-Willingham House and in the early 1980s was moved from its original location to the Georgia Agrirama, a living history museum in Tifton. The completely restored home features beautiful heart pine, expertly shaped and carved by the shipbuilders from Connecticut.

Meanwhile, another South Carolinian named Irvine Walker Myers would be permanently "transplanted" to this part of Georgia. In 1894, the eighteen-year-old left Pamplico, South Carolina, and eventually found work in Tifton as a desk clerk at the Hotel Sadie. The "Sadie" (named for the daughter of the builder, J. L. Phillips) was a favorite haunt for weary train travelers and a local gathering place for dances, poetry readings, and plays. The hotel was rare for the time because it had fifty guest rooms. Irvine's ineffable charm, good looks, and strong work ethic soon paid off when he became part owner of the Hotel Sadie. In time, Irvine would meet and fall in love with Pearl Willingham, Bessie Willingham Tift's youngest sibling. The couple married in a beautiful formal ceremony in Atlanta, in December of 1899.

Made of wood, the Hotel Sadie was completely destroyed by fire in 1905. With the financial backing of his new in-laws, Irvine Myers built a grand and beautiful brick hotel where the Hotel Sadie once stood. With a whopping $135,000 price tag, exorbitant for early 1900s, Irvine Myers wanted a suitable name for the new hotel. He decided to have a contest to name the hotel and the winner would be treated to a weekend's free stay. It would be the local superior court judge, the Honorable Raleigh Eve, who would come up with the name Myon, stemming from the first two letters in Myers and the last two in Tifton. The name thus settled, the grand opening was celebrated in 1906.

Affectionately known by family and close friends as "Brother," Henry Tift Myers was born to Irvine and Pearl Myers on September 16, 1907. He and his sister Marguerite (older by three years) lived in the stately Hotel Myon. Not far away from their downtown residence, Pearl and Irvine owned over 1000 acres of idyllic farmland that ensured lazy days and healthy outdoor adventure for their children. Gracing the land the Myers family once owned is the second largest known magnolia tree in the nation.

Pearl doted on her son, Henry, and he could tease and charm his mother into getting him just about anything that he wanted. Marguerite was her father's

Pearl and Marguerite Myers

Pearl and Irvine circa 1899

Hotel Myon - Tifton, Georgia

Bob Hawthorne seems dwarfed by the (presumed) second largest magnolia tree in the nation. Today the tree stands at Tifton's Industrial Park - property once owned by Irvine and Pearl Myers. *The News Examiner*, March 26, 1970.

"baby girl" and good luck charm. Irvine never went to a tobacco market opening without her—he claimed that she was the reason he got good prices for his tobacco. Irvine had introduced the lucrative cash crop to South Georgia, having gained experience in the tobacco markets of South Carolina.

Pearl learned to be a good businesswoman and informed investor, always perusing the stock reports first in the newspaper. She enjoyed making money, but not spending it, and she was always looking for new business opportunities. It appears that in 1916 Pearl and a couple of her friends tried their hand in the herbal remedy or snake oil business so popular at the time. Found in the May 1916 issue of *The Tifton Gazette* is Pearl's application for incorporation:

> The particular business which they propose
> to engage in and carry on in the name of said
> corporation will be to manufacture a certain
> remedy for Indigestion known as Conger's C-I-
> C and sell the same also to manufacture other
> remedies and medicines and to sell drugs of any
> nature and kind in compliance with the laws of

said State.

This venture, soon abandoned, was not a tremendous success, but never mind; there would be many more business opportunities for this industrious, hard-working, no-nonsense woman. Pearl was unlike her many sisters, who were ladylike, reserved and regularly attended church. Compared to them, she was a renegade. Pearl, who could be attractive enough when she dressed up, did not care much for adorning herself because she was too busy working and making money to waste time on her appearance. Always received by and comfortable with the local businessmen, Pearl was part of the good ol' boys' network. If the occasion called for it, this well-bred woman could let the obscenities fly and she always had a bottle of bourbon stashed in the trunk of her Cadillac to bring out for "serious" conversations. Everyone in town knew about her fast driving. Again, quoting from *The Tifton Gazette*—July 1919:

> Of the victims of the automobile collision
> Tuesday night, all were doing very well this
> morning. Mrs. Myers was resting well and Mrs.

Wilkes and Mrs. Smith are fast recovering. Mr. Williams is carrying some big bruises and Mr. Baker was reported as getting along all right.

It was often said that Henry Tift Myers got his love of speed from his mother. While Pearl was driving to Atlanta on State Highway 41, somewhere around Chula, Georgia, she was pulled over for speeding. Aggravated by his audacity for stopping her, Pearl told the young officer, "go ahead and give me a ticket for my return trip and save us both the trouble." Years later while driving to her hotel (The Ocean View) on St. Simons Island, Georgia, Pearl lost control of her car while speeding around a curve. Fortunately, only her leg was broken from the crash. And then there was the occasion when she ran her new Cadillac into one of her downtown Tifton buildings, taking out a large chunk of bricks. The police officer, upon arriving, was told: "Sonny, this is my car and this is my building and if I want to drive my car into my building, I will." (In Pearl's defense, this incident was before the government standardized the shift pattern of automatic transmissions. She had previously been driving a Chrysler that had a different shift pattern from her new Cadillac.)

The tobacco buyers from the north enjoyed the fine quail hunting offered in South Georgia. For those who would rather hunt golf balls, Irvine and other Tifton businessmen constructed a golf course. The buyers were treated like royalty and loved their sojourns in Tifton. The opening of the tobacco market was hailed as the social event of the year and it was a tradition for the out-of-towners to stay at the Hotel Myon where the accommodations, cuisine, and hospitality were simply the best.

Beginning around 1914, Irvine and Pearl came to know and love the unusual, eccentric, and unconventional Chase Salmon Osborn. This former governor of Michigan stayed many times at the Hotel Myon while traveling the country by railway. He later acquired "Possum Polk," a cabin in nearby Poulan, Georgia, where he enjoyed staying during the winter months. For those who want to know more about this explorer, adventurer, politician, writer, publisher, speaker, and environmentalist (along with numerous other descriptions), his autobiography, *The*

Henry Tift Myers Circa 1910

Marguerite and "Brother" in front of the Hotel Myon, circa 1916.

"Brother" and Marguerite

Iron Hunter, written in 1919, is now back in print. Always one for doing the unexpected, Chase adopted his secretary and changed her name from Stella Brunt to Stellanova (new star) Osborn. Two days before his death, he had the adoption annulled and married Stellanova (his first wife died in 1948.) Chase Osborn was a friend of the Myers family until his death in 1949. He followed the career of Henry Tift Myers and wrote articles about his aviation accomplishments and sent copies to Pearl. In his autobiography, he mentions South Georgia, his bungalow at Possum Polk and belonging to "a little club of close, fine friends." Generous in nature, he gave away over 800 acres of uncut forest that he owned to establish a Boy Scout camp in South Georgia. Chase Salmon Osborn—an amazing character.

It was apparent early on that Henry Tift Myers was quick to learn and his parents decided that he, along with his sister Marguerite, would be schooled in Atlanta. The large city offered greater opportunities for the children and Pearl, never fearing a challenge, moved with them and bought a house on Piedmont Avenue. Irvine stayed in Tifton to run the businesses. By this time, in addition to the hotel and tobacco warehouses, he operated a large farm and was an officer in a Tifton bank, along with various other business endeavors.

Unlike his wife, Pearl, who attended Cox College in Atlanta, Irvine did not take advantage of a formal education and he lived to regret it. Irvine's father had graduated from Furman University and more than likely encouraged Irvine to attend college but he was young and adventuresome and wanted to strike out on his own. Now that he was a father, he was determined that his children would take advantage of an education and it would be the best one that he could provide.

Marguerite graduated from a private Atlanta girl's school, Washington Seminary, in 1923. (This is the same school Margaret Mitchell, the famed author of *Gone With The Wind*, had attended a few years earlier. Established in 1878 by two grandnieces of George Washington, it was housed in what is considered to be the largest home ever built on Peachtree Street. In 1953, the school merged with Westminster Schools and the house was subsequently destroyed.)

Henry attended Atlanta's Tech High School that opened in 1909. In addition to a fine academic curriculum, the school offered practical and useful vocational training. (Grady High School now stands at this location.)

Based on letters written by Pearl to her husband in Tifton, it seems that young Henry discovered girls while in Atlanta and lost interest in his schoolwork. Not only

Boy's High/Tech High, circa 1922

25

Marguerite Myers

Pearl and her children vacation in the North Georgia mountains, circa 1910.

Red Cross exhibit Atlanta, Georgia. Circa 1917. Marguerite is third from left.

Marguerite Myers vacationing in Miami. Circa 1925

was he "girl crazy," he was not as respectful to his mother and sister as a young man should be. Irvine Myers would never allow that kind of behavior and in 1922, he sent a stringent ten-page letter to Henry telling him to straighten up or else. Excerpts from the letter are shown below:

> My Dear Boy,
>
> I would much rather see you and talk to you than write you, but as it is not convenient for me to go up there, I am going to write—
>
> When last I was up there I could see that you were more interested in other things than your home and your studies. Now I am not going to write a fussy letter nor tell you all I think, but just want to ask you to do some thinking, real honest thinking and see if you think you are giving us a square deal.
>
> Nothing will fit you for life like an education and a determination to be something and both of these are strictly up to you, money cannot buy either unless you do your part. I have decided definitely that unless you become more interested in your studies and take better advantages of the opportunities offered you there, I am going to take you away from Atlanta and put you in a small town boarding school. You will have many, many temptations but if you have the stuff in you, you can overcome them all, if you cannot overcome them, then it is best for you to get away where these temptations are not.
>
> If you will take more interest in the home (keep the yard clean) be more thoughtful of Mother and Sister and keep up your studies, you will be much happier and they will be too. Write me what you think and when I do get there we will talk it over. With much love to you all (kiss Mother and Sister for me) Your Devoted, Daddy

Irvine Myers was loving and kind but steadfast in his decisions. He followed through on his warning and Henry soon found himself attending Culver Military Academy in Culver, Indiana. To Irvine's relief, this nipped Henry's problematic behavior. Culver Military Academy focused on character and leadership. Founded in 1894 by Henry Harrison Culver "for the purpose of thoroughly preparing young men for the best colleges, scientific schools and businesses of America," the academy proudly lists among its graduates actor Hal Holbrook as well as former CEOs of Pepsi Cola Company and the Campbell Soup Company. The academy's position on character reads in part:

> Sound judgment is not by itself sufficient for moral action; for a person may be prevented from doing what they know is right by their inclinations to do otherwise. For example, they may find that emotion overcomes their best efforts to chart rational courses of action. Hence, the importance of the virtue of courage, for courageous persons are able to do what they know is right even when their feelings draw them in other directions. They have, as we say, the courage of their convictions. The bodily appetites, basic to all human beings, can also deflect attention away from a rational desire to do the good. Herein lies the significance of the virtue of moderation, for moderate persons are individuals in whom the bodily passions have been educated to play an appropriate role in a balanced life.

Irvine Myers lived this kind of philosophy and was proud when his son graduated from Culver Military Academy, in 1925. While at Culver, Henry participated in football, basketball, baseball, soccer, and track. He also won a medal for automatic rifle. Many years later when Henry had difficulty with his only child, Tift, he would try the same military school remedy on him. Unfortunately, Culver Military Academy, Sewanee Military Academy and Schriner Military Institute all failed to deliver the hoped-for results. It would take something other than military schools to straighten out Tift.

The University of Georgia in Athens was Henry's next logical step for his college education. His extracurricular activities there included the football team (fullback), SAE fraternity, boxing, and dating many beautiful college girls. A local clothing store in Athens supplied him with wonderful clothes to wear as their walking advertisement. He loved to dress and clothes looked great on his lean 5' 10" frame.

Henry writes to Marguerite on this photograph: "To 'Old Lady' the best friend I've ever had. With my best regards, Brother."

Henry Tift Myers, Culver Military Academy, circa 1925.

For those who know football, two of his teammates were Herdis McCrary (Green Bay Packers) and all-time Georgia football letterman, Bennie Rothstein. These guys were ahead of Henry in size, strength and speed. Thrilling moments in an important game were not to be his. Nevertheless, one of his coaches said of him: "He never missed a practice, never lost his ambition, never skimped on a tackle, never failed to drive his hardest. Not only did he inspire his fellow players, he inspired his coaches too."

The most spectacular events of the 1929 football season included the dedication of Sanford Stadium and the defeat of Yale, 15 to 0. The Georgia / Georgia Tech game would long be remembered as well. Quoting from *The History of the University of Georgia* by Thomas Walter Reed:

> Playing in Athens to a crowd of more than 20,000 in a driving rainstorm, Georgia was victorious with a score of 12 to 6. After the game, fans raided all of the dry good stores and completely cleaned them out of socks, stockings, underwear, shirts, ladies dresses, raincoats, and the like. Mud was everywhere from Athens to Atlanta. Automobiles, bumper to bumper, crawled along the seventy miles and it was reliably reported that one farmer had to wait an hour

before he could cross the road and milk his cow.

Henry finished the football season and completed his studies, majoring in commerce and French. Unbeknownst to Henry, becoming familiar with the French language would come in very handy in the years to come. He graduated in 1929 and it was in Athens that he first learned to fly.

When he first experienced the thrill of flight, did he have any idea what destiny held for him? Did he even dream that one day he would be the airplane pilot for presidents and kings, visit fifty-six countries, set aviation records, and actually be where history was being made? Watching the derring-do of barnstorming pilots when he was a child must have fueled the dreams of the small-town Georgia boy. Years later in newspaper interviews, Henry would mention those pilots he saw as a child. He said he thought he could do what they were doing and he thought it was great that they got to sit down the whole time. His success at flying, he said with a grin, was based on the simple fact that he was "born lazy."

At first, Henry's parents were not supportive of his interest in flying. Although they could have supplied him with flying lessons and an airplane, they chose not to do so. To get around this obstacle, he started boxing professionally subrosa. He used an assumed name and earned about fifty bucks a fight. Little did his parents

Henry as a University of Georgia football player. Pandora 1929.

D.H. ANSLEY   F.C. DUBLEY *   CRAIG BARROW JR   R.G. HOOKS   A.A. LAWRENCE JR.   LATHROP MITCHELL   F.D. RUSSELL

S.C. COX JR.   H.M. LOKEY JR.   F.M. SKINNER   R.S. CLEMMONS   S.L. UPSON JR.   J.A. JOHNSON   M.P. JARNAGIN III

W.I. BURTON   H.T. MYERS   J.E. PALMOUR JR.   R.D. FEAGIN   H.C. STELLING   B.S. WALKER   J.C. OLIVER

G.F. CRISFIELD   G.D. BRANTLEY   F.G. LUMPKIN   J.L. HOUSTON   B.P. WOLFF   N.W. JONES   S.M. WELLBORN

T.W. VENTULETT   J.W. MADDOX   M.H. COX   J.W. GARLAND   L.F. HOLLAND   T.H. LOKEY   J.T. BEESON

A.C. MOBLEY JR.   J.P. VENTULETT   R.M. TIMMONS   A.B. RUSSELL   R.B. ROSE   J.W. McINTIRE   J.B. GORDON

M.H. GORDON III   M.P. BARROW   J.A. BOYKIN JR.   J.E. FEAGIN   S.R. HEYS   LINDSEY HOPKINS JR.   J.A. WADE   H.M. WALKER

Henry's fraternity, Sigma Alpha Epsilon, University of Georgia. Pandora 1929.

Henry and college friend tour the West Coast, circa 1928.

Right, Henry and unidentified friend on a hunting trip, circa 1930.

Janet B. (last name unknown), Fred G. Hodgson, Jr., Henry and Josephine Bell, circa 1930.

Left to right: Janet (last name unknown), Henry and Josephine Bell, Panacea, Florida circa 1930.

know he was slugging it out in the boxing ring. They thought that he was selling bonds to earn his money.

A well-known boxer around this time was William Lawrence "Young" Stribling who lived in Macon, Georgia. Sharing the interest of boxing and the love of flying, he and Henry became friends. When Henry was able, he purchased a small plane from the great boxer, Stribling. There was no turning back now; Henry's flying career had begun in earnest. Tragically, Stribling was killed in a motorcycle crash when he was only twenty-eight years old. He was inducted into the Boxing Hall of Fame in 1996 and is considered one of the greatest feint artists of all time. Stribling's biographer, Jimmy Jones, who covered hundreds of his fights, said that what set him apart from other boxers was "his exemplary conduct both in the ring and out and a strict code of ethics, flawless character, self discipline, modesty, a Christian attitude toward opponents, and the highest degree of sportsmanship." To read more about this wonderful role model and his colorful family, there is a book called *The King of the Canebrakes* by the aforementioned Jimmy Jones that is available at some public libraries in Georgia.

When Irvine and Pearl realized that flying was their son's reason for being, they yielded with one condition— he must receive the best flight training available. And the best training at that time would be at Kelly Field in San Antonio, Texas, and Selfridge Field in Michigan. Henry obviously worked hard and completed the Army Air Corps training, graduating at the top of his class in 1932.

In April of that same year, his sister, Marguerite, married Andrew Roy Miller of Bethesda, Maryland. After Marguerite graduated from Washington Seminary in Atlanta, she attended a fashion college in New York where she learned to design and sew clothing, something she would enjoy doing the rest of her life. It is not clear where she met Roy Miller, but at twenty-eight-years-old she was approaching what some considered old maid status and decided to marry. Pearl Myers did not care much for Roy Miller as her new son-in-law but tried to make the best of the situation. Marguerite settled down with Roy in their home in Maryland. She could not have children and that was probably for the best because of her controlling and stern personality. Much to her delight, in a few years, an unusual turn of events would have the brother she loved so much living in close proximity to her in the Washington, D.C. area.

After his training and services were completed with the Army Air Corps, Henry relocated to Fort Worth, Texas, home of American Airlines, in hopes of getting a job with the airline. It was the height of the Depression and the only job available was as clerk at their Dallas office. He took the job and not long afterward there was a flu epidemic that had many of the American pilots out on sick leave. A supervisor with American asked in desperation, "Can anybody fly one of these planes?" Quick as a flash, up went Henry's hand and in January of 1933 he began flying as co-pilot with American Airlines. Not long afterward, he earned his captain's wings.

Before he was made captain and while he flew as a co-pilot with Capt. Andy Andrews, they set a flying record, making a 3000-mile hop from California to New York in eleven hours and twenty-four minutes. They then stopped long enough in Washington, D.C., to deliver orchids (cut earlier that day in California) to first lady Eleanor Roosevelt. In a few short years, Henry would meet the first lady again and have the honor and responsibility of flying her all over the world as presidential pilot.

In October of 1937, Irvine Myers traveled from Georgia up to Tennessee to board one of his son's flights. "It was the thrill of a life-time," he wrote in a letter to his wife. Sadly, Pearl received the letter in Tifton the very day Irvine died. Always an immaculate dresser and neat in appearance, he wanted to get a haircut before returning home to Tifton. While at a barbershop in Nashville, Tennessee, he suffered a massive heart attack and died. (Ironically, Irvine and his son Henry would both die from heart disease at the same age of sixty-one). Because he always had such high hopes and aspirations for his son, it was a shame that Irvine did not live long enough to see them materialize. These kind words were written about Irvine Myers in the book *The History of Tift County*:

> Few have been possessed of a personality, which so endeared them to a host of friends, as was Irvine W. Myers. Exceptionally handsome, possessed of a rich

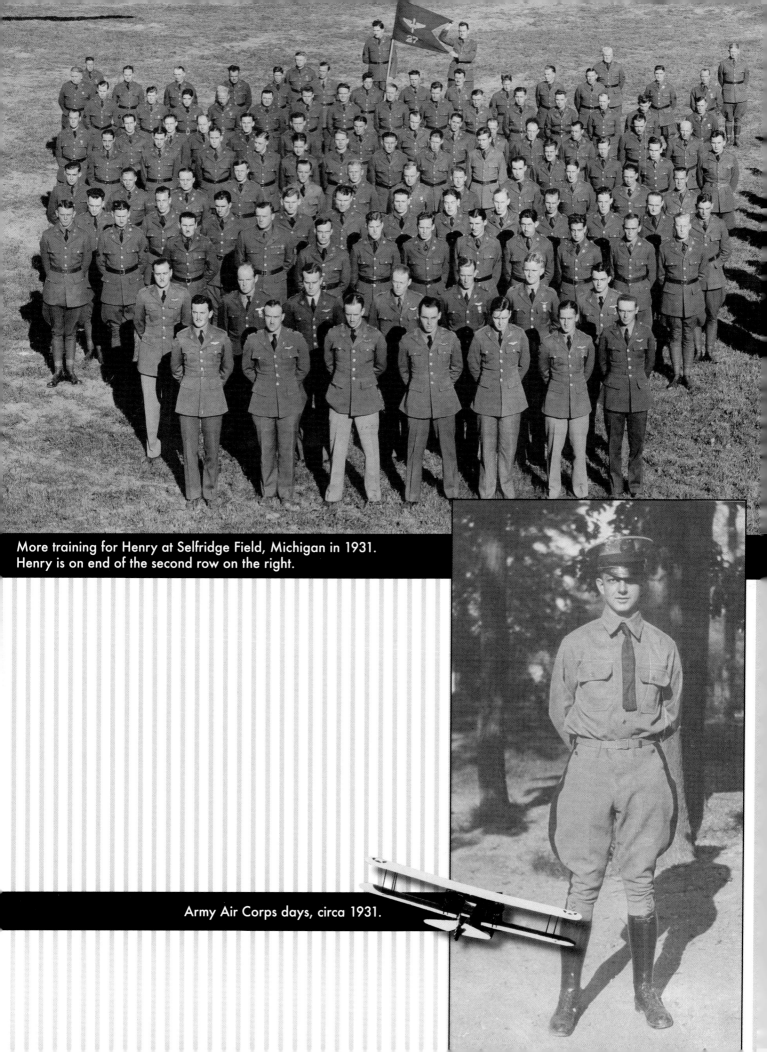

More training for Henry at Selfridge Field, Michigan in 1931.
Henry is on end of the second row on the right.

Army Air Corps days, circa 1931.

and sonorous voice and with a kind friendliness, he numbered his friends by those who knew him. When he died a community wept.

In loving, detailed letters to his mother, Henry kept her posted on his "comings and goings" and the state of his finances. Being very thrifty and a prudent businessman (lessons he learned from his mother), even in the 1930s he had substantial savings and sent Marguerite fifty dollars each month from his paycheck. He was able to buy a $3,500 boat and loved to cruise around Lake Worth and Eagle Mountain Lake. Boating would become another great love in Henry's life, as would fast cars and a beautiful Fort Worth, Texas, debutante named Maidee Williams.

Maidee, the daughter of Henry Washington Williams and Maidee Calloway Williams, was a sweet, beautiful, and vivacious girl. Her father was a successful businessman and owned a wholesale pharmaceutical company in Fort Worth. Her only sibling, a sister named Elizabeth, was killed in 1912 at the age of six in a fireworks accident. Maidee, born in 1917, was the center of her parent's life and successfully spoiled.

After attending Mrs. Semple's School for Girls in New York, Maidee returned to Fort Worth and was a familiar face on the social pages of the *Fort Worth Star-Telegram*. What times she had! Young, beautiful, and eager for life,

she ran away and married a wealthy Texas oilman. Her parents, thinking she was too young, quickly and quietly had the brief and unsanctioned marriage annulled. To this day, many old friends of the family in Fort Worth have never known about this short liaison. Single again and back in the social flow of things, Maidee went out for a game of tennis at Colonial Country Club in Fort Worth. On the tennis court, the Fort Worth beauty was introduced to a slow talking, handsome American Airlines pilot who possessed a Georgia-born charm. In time, Texas and Georgia would "merge" when Maidee Calloway Williams became Mrs. Henry Tift Myers.

Their easy flow of life in Fort Worth was disrupted by the attack in 1941 on Pearl Harbor. Like everyone else, Henry's life was changed forever. He was ordered to leave American Airlines and to go back into the Army Air Corps. In this short memo written on May 16, 1942, to American Airlines he gives notice:

> This is to advise that I have been ordered to report to the Commanding General, U.S. Army Air Forces for duty with the Air Force Ferrying Command, Washington, D.C. It is requested, therefore, that I be granted a leave of absence effective May 16, in accordance with section 25, paragraph 1 of the Pilot's Agreement."
>
> —Henry T. Myers

Maidee Williams, Fort Worth Debutante, 1937. Rhea-Engert Studio.

Hank Myers, American Airlines, 1934.

Maidee Calloway Williams.

Hank Myers in front of his 1937 Cord 812 Phaeton.

In a hastily written letter to his mother in 1942, Henry told her he had just gotten his military orders. He knew that the orders were for something special but he could not yet reveal to her what they were. "I would like to marry Maidee before I leave but my better judgment says NO. I know I'll be back anyway and the war should be over soon now that I'm in (Ha! Ha!)." Continuing the letter, Henry writes:

I go into the army as a 1st Lt. but should be promoted rather rapidly as I am being called for some sort of special mission the nature of which I could not disclose if I knew. I do not know yet where I'll go first but possibly Miami and if so, I'll be able to stop by the house. I'll let you know if not forbidden as soon as I know. This is all very sudden I know and we do not quite understand it but if they need us more elsewhere than they do the airlines, I am ready and anxious. I have no fear and I'm glad that now the uncertainty as to what I'm going to do is over. Well must get a nap now as am dead tired. I hate to bring you this news but I am not

worrying and I hope you won't.

In his characteristically tender way, Henry reassured his mother and let her know that he was up for the task at hand. Upon receiving his letter, Pearl Myers immediately fired off the following Western Union telegram to an assistant for Georgia Senator Walter Franklin George.

(Senator George served in the United States Senate from 1922 until 1957— the Walter F. George School of Law at Mercer University, in Macon, Georgia is named in his honor.)

The following reply was sent from Senator George's assistant, Christie Bell Kennedy, on May 18, 1942. (Originally from Tifton, Christie Bell knew all of the

Myers family and was happy to welcome Henry Myers to Washington. Christie Bell later served as clerk of the Foreign Relations Committee and then Senator George named her as clerk of the Finance Committee, the first woman ever to serve in that capacity.)

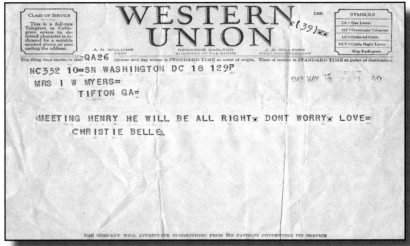

The sensible and practical Henry rented his house in Fort Worth to an elderly couple for seventy dollars a month, sold one of his cars, and put the boat in storage. He and his future bride, Maidee, must have worked out some kind of "understanding" about seeing other people, considering their impending separation.

Henry's life prior to this time had been systematically planned for success, from his satisfying childhood and first-rate education to his rewarding flying career and his relationship with a wealthy Texas beauty. Yes, Irvine Myers would be pleased thus far with his son. Henry was now thirty-five years old and more handsome that ever. He was about to embark on the journey of his life and his earlier accolades would be left in the dust. In no way was he ready for commitments on the home front. Miss Maidee Calloway Williams would just have to wait and he hoped that she would.

"I'm leaving things in good shape in Ft. Worth," read Henry's last line to his mother in May of 1942. With husband Irvine gone, Pearl alone had to bear the incredible apprehension she felt for her son. Fortunately, she knew just what to do to ease her worried mind. She would stay busy—very busy. Pearl always found peace and comfort in hard work. The fact that she made a lot of money in the process was only secondary to her absolute joy and delight in good, honest labor.

Pearl Myers serving buttermilk to the tobacco buyers—some of them preferred her bourbon.

CRUISING
ALTITUDE

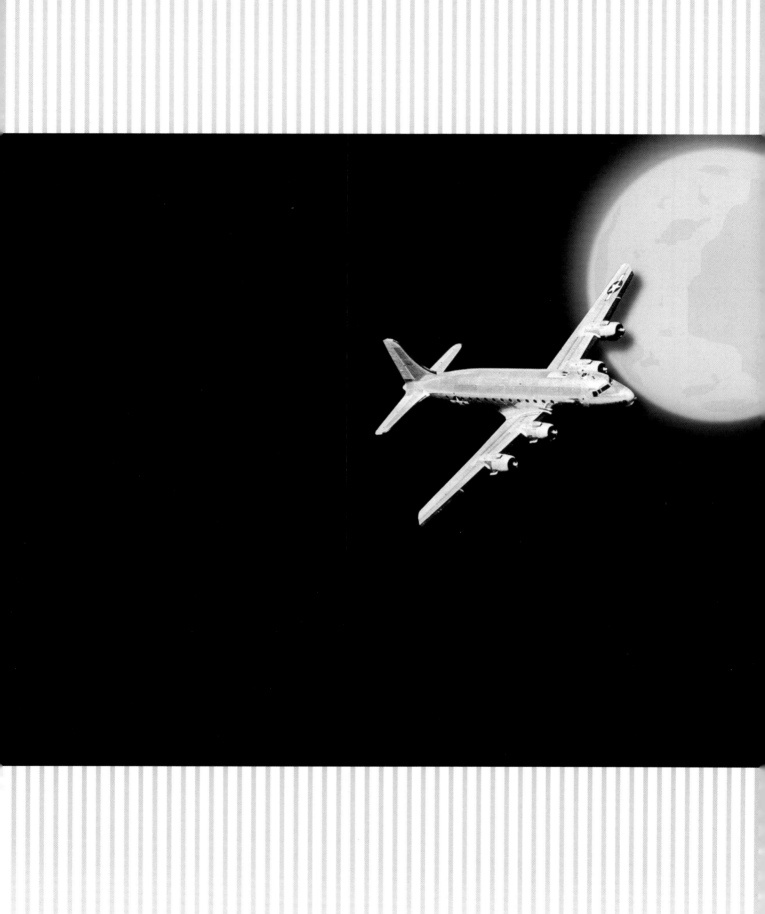

In the coming years, Pearl would make notes at the top of Henry's letters to her explaining *ex post facto* the nature of the particular mission he was not allowed to discuss with her at the time. He would write, "I can't tell you now who I am with or where we are going, but you will know when you read about it in the papers." So, interestingly enough, Pearl was privy to historical events before they happened, although she did not know exactly what or who they involved.

A notation written on the outside of a War Department envelope postmarked September 16, 1942, in Pearl's robust handwriting states: "I treasure this letter above words." The letter reads in part:

Subject: Love from Bro

To: Dear Moms:

> Just a note to send my love and let you know that I am not going on the trip I told you I was going on. Sis seemed to think you were worried about it so thought I had better let you know, at once, I'm not going. Gen. George and I were going to England for a conference but it is off for now anyway. Well, today is my birthday and as always, I am grateful to my moms for putting me here and seeing to it that I grew up and became endowed with so many things for which I am ever thankful. I have always felt that I am the

> luckiest of mortals and most of that luck, my precious, has come from being your son and having you to see to it that my feet were turned and guided along the narrow paths. I can't say that I have always treaded the right paths (by any means) but I can say that whenever I have deviated, it has not been your fault. Will write again soon—hope you are taking care of yourself even if you have to close down the hotel.

> Most devotedly, Bro

Henry was a charmer with all of his women. He knew the right words to say and when to say them. It was around 1942 that he began seeing a couple of Hollywood starlets. It was only a short drive to Hollywood from the Douglas plant where the planes were serviced and what else was there for him to do while he was waiting? Maidee also had her own Hollywood connections through her uncle, Sam Calloway, an executive with United Artists Film Company.

Henry once shared an apartment with Douglas Fairbanks, Jr., in Algiers. President Roosevelt had appointed Fairbanks as a special envoy; the sharing of the apartment was either arranged through the army or by Henry's connections with the starlets. Whatever the reason, bunking with a Hollywood star of that caliber

Hank (kneeling in dark coat behind Gen. George) and others surround Olivia de Havilland. 1942

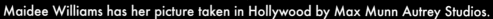

Maidee Williams has her picture taken in Hollywood by Max Munn Autrey Studios.

Hank (left) appears to be speaking with Bette Davis on the set of *In This Our Life* (General George is to her left) 1942

TIME

THE WEEKLY NEWSMAGAZINE

AIR TRANSPORT'S GENERAL GEORGE
The skyways of war will be flown by wings of peace.
(Army & Navy)

Gen. Harold S. George

C. R. Smith attended Maidee and Hank's wedding in 1945. Associated Press Photo.

General George, seated, and Hank Myers, to his left, look over maps. 1942

would be an extraordinary experience for most. Henry thought of Fairbanks as just another "regular Joe."

Henry's first assignment after being called back into the Army Air Corps from American Airlines was aide and pilot for Gen. Harold S. George, Commanding General, Air Transport Command. This was four months after the bombing of Pearl Harbor.

American Airlines President and CEO Cyrus Rowlett (C.R.) Smith had recommended Henry to General George, saying that he was an "ace pilot." During World War II, C.R. Smith left his position at American Airlines and helped organize the Air Transport Command, a division of the Army Air Corps, serving as deputy commander with Gen. Harold George and finally as a major general. After the war was over, C.R. returned to American Airlines and in 1968 President Lyndon Johnson appointed him as United States Secretary of Commerce. Not one for bureaucracy, C.R. returned to American Airlines in 1973 but retired less than a year later because he felt that he was "working in a 747 era with a DC-6 state of mind."

Coincidentally, a 1931 newspaper article shows a picture of Maidee, as a bridesmaid in the C.R. Smith wedding. Maidee knew the president of American Airlines before Henry worked at American Airlines and before she knew Henry. Fourteen years later, C.R. Smith would attend the small wedding ceremony for Hank and Maidee.

Also a bit of a coincidence, President Roosevelt's son, Elliott, was a groomsman in the C.R. Smith wedding. Elliott lived in Texas and knew Maidee. He worked for the Hearst radio chain and when America entered the war, he joined the Army Air Corps. Hank Myers would have the solemn duty of bringing Elliott home from London for President Roosevelt's funeral.

At the time, Henry did not know exactly what was in store for him as an aide for General George. All he knew was that he just wanted to continue to fly. "But I don't want to be a general's aide," Henry said to his boss at American Airlines. "You can tell that to the general," C.R. answered dryly. Henry did voice his objections to the general, "I've seen what aides have to do—please sir, find somebody else." "You like to fly don't you?" asked General George. "Yes sir, I do!" "Well, then, keep your shirt on; you'll like this job." That was certainly an understatement. Henry Tift Myers got the best job in the war, if there was such a thing. Hank Myers always had the highest regard for C. R. Smith and felt that it was because of his recommendation to General George that he was selected as the first presidential pilot.

This pilot was not the only one in his family that took to the skies and had an unusual career. Henry's beautiful cousin, Nedra Harrison Anageros, learned how to fly in Tifton and trained with aviatrix Col. Jacqueline Cochran at Avenger Field in Sweetwater, Texas, in the spring of 1943. This group of women became the famed female military pilots of World War II.

Nedra's grandmother, Florence Willingham Pickard, was another one of Pearl's older sisters and her grandfather, Dr. William Lowndes Pickard, was the president of Mercer University during World War I. Nedra, known as Kewpie to her friends, grew up in Tifton where she was pretty and popular—she was selected as Miss Tifton High School. Although flying was uncommon for women at the time, that is not the only thing that set her apart from the norm. In Nedra's own words:

> I had left Tifton and gone to Emerson College in Boston. To help pay
> expenses, I had begun modeling some. Later, I went to New York hoping for a
> career in the theater, but was modeling in the meantime. Unfortunately, there
> weren't many modeling jobs in the late 1930s for those with my looks. I had
> dark hair and a French-Oriental look. It was the All American girls who were
> in demand. One day, my agent called and said, 'Nedra, I think your exotic
> good looks are going to pay off' and told me to come in. It seems that the
> artist/cartoonist Milton Caniff had been looking for a model and could not
> find exactly the 'look' he wanted. He had a preconceived notion, a Eurasian
> look, I went to see him and when I walked in, he was looking at a big photo
> of me. He looked up as I came in and said, 'there she is—that's my Dragon
> Lady—she even has the dimple in her chin.'

That is how Henry's cousin Nedra Harrison Anageros became the model for Dragon

Nedra Harrison, as a Powers model in New York.
The Daily Tifton Gazette, February 9, 1980.

Beautiful Nedra Harrison, the aviatrix, 1942.
The Daily Tifton Gazette, February 9, 1980.

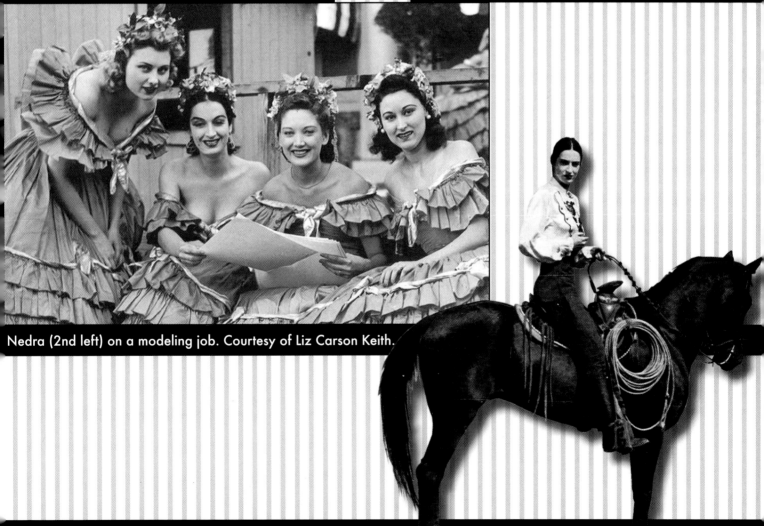

Nedra (2nd left) on a modeling job. Courtesy of Liz Carson Keith.

The elegant and graceful Nedra Harrison performed on horse-back with the quadrille at the New York World's Fair in 1939. Courtesy of Liz Carson Keith.

Lady in the famed cartoon strip *Terry and the Pirates*. An article in *Yankee* magazine noted: "By 1940 the Dragon Lady was the nation's leading animation figure and every male reader from age thirteen to 103 had fallen quite in love with her."

Nedra became a member of the Women Fliers of America in New York and Pennsylvania to log more solo time. She was invited to train for the Cochran group at Avenger Field; but before Nedra completed the full flight course, she learned that her husband was returning home from overseas. She decided to drop out of the flight program so that she could be with him. Nedra is mentioned in the book *Those Wonderful Women in Their Flying Machines* written by Sally Keil and once posed for Salvador Dali for his painting "Madonna of the Sea." During the New York World's Fair in 1939, she rode the Quadrille (equestrian macramé in Latin—when mounted teams perform intricate and beautiful interfacing patterns, like a military drill team) on horseback in the Wild West Rodeo.

Marguerite and Nedra remained close throughout their lives and in 1969, Henry's son, Tift Myers, went to her home in San Francisco for a visit and found her still beautiful and gracious. She loved to scuba dive and had become a licensed cytologist. Her husband, Spiro Anageros, was a well-known sculptor and their home

was filled with his beautiful art. The author of this book contacted Nedra in the spring of 2004 for permission to include her pictures in this book and found her to be absolutely delightful. Sadly, Nedra passed away on September 20, 2004, at the age of eighty-eight. Her sizable estate ($3 million) was left to Mercer University.

From the very beginning, General George changed the way Henry conducted his flying procedures. Being very methodical and always planning for every contingency in advance was Henry's style. "I never flew anywhere without knowing the full details of the weather, exact load of gas, weight of plane and passengers and I always had a detailed flight plan, but General George changed all that," Henry explained in an interview.

The Air Transport Command was considered a people mover rather than a supply carrier, and flying a C-87 that had to be ready and on call to fly VIPs and VVIPs (four stars and above) any place in the world on short notice was Henry's job under General George. Oftentimes, this required Henry to fly to the front lines of battle.

Henry's first flight with his unpredictable boss began with a phone call from the general at 1 a.m. telling him to be at Bolling Field for a 4 a.m. takeoff. "Where to, General?" Henry asked. "Presque Isle," the general ordered. "Yessir," was Henry's answer in his best military manner, but what he really wanted to say was, "Where

Left to right, Milton Caniff, Nedra and Bud Davis (also known as Pat Ryan, he-man extraordinaire). Nedra once praised Caniff for his "outstanding work" and for "being an absolutely marvelous person. You know, he is a very outstanding artist, not just a creator of comic strips." Quote from *The Daily Tifton Gazette*, illustration from *Look Magazine*, 1940.

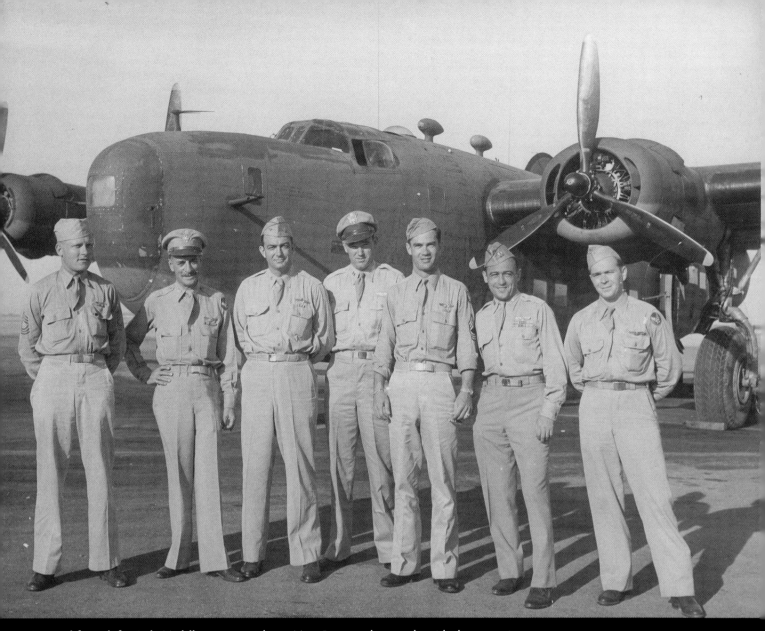

Second from left, Col. Middleton, an aide to Mrs. Roosevelt, stands with the crew in front of the *Guess Where II*.

King George of Greece and Hank discuss the *Sacred Cow* (the king flew in his underwear).

the hell is that?" Quickly, Henry arrived at Bolling Field, where he grabbed an armload of maps, climbed on the plane, spread the maps around the cabin and had just found that Presque Isle was in Maine, when the general climbed aboard. "Let's go," General George ordered. "Yessir," Henry said, feeling very secure in his new knowledge. "But not to Presque Isle—to Ottawa," said the general. At least Henry knew that Ottawa was to the North. He quickly worked out a route, got weather data through complicated army wartime procedures, and delivered the general to Ottawa.

After that ordeal, the worn-out pilot was looking forward to some sack time because he had not slept in three days. But while at the airport, they met New York Mayor Fiorello La Guardia. He was fuming because there was no plane to take him home. "Why, Myers will be glad to run you down in my plane," 'Generous' General George said. Henry was not overjoyed but tried to appear so. He learned to expect the general's penchant for last-minute changes and because of this characteristic, Henry and the general's assistant, Rex Smith, christened the general's first plane *The Sudden Notion*. The next

plane was named *Guess Where* and its successor was called *Guess Where II*. The *Guess Where* was the plane that mysteriously vanished on a clear day in the mid-Pacific in March of 1945 with Lt. Gen. Millard F. Harmon and top members of his staff. Henry had a theory that the plane blew up and once said: "The *Guess Where* leaked gasoline onto the flight deck—somebody lit a cigarette at the wrong time and that was all."

It has been said that Henry Tift Myers flew more top brass and world leaders than any other pilot to date. That is why he was referred to in magazine articles as "The Pilot of the Brass Hat Squadron."

In July 1942, Henry was given the order to fly King George II of Greece on a four-day tour within the United States. The plans were for Henry and the crew to pick up the king in New York City and take him to various places of interest in Buffalo, Detroit, Cleveland, Washington D.C., and, finally, back to New York City. The co-pilot for the first part of the trip was a stuffy colonel who immediately wanted to call the State Department for the rules of protocol for flying royalty. The colonel wanted to know specifically: "Who should enter the plane first—he or the king?" Henry told him, "Forget it—whoever gets to the plane first can just climb on." While the colonel was busy calling the State Department about "kingly" protocol, Henry met the king, escorted him onto the plane and was ready to go. Certainly a modicum of decorum was used with the king, but Henry's easy-going and friendly nature many times was the best judgment call. In a little while, after take off, Henry turned around to see King George II standing at the door of the cockpit in his underwear! It was a hot July day—they were flying low because of head winds and there was no altitude to cool off. In perfect Oxford English, the king explained that it was much cooler that way and that his uniform would not be wrinkled. From that point on, everyone relaxed and enjoyed the casual atmosphere—even the crew stripped down to their drawers! After each one of the landings, the king would come forward and congratulate Henry on the smooth handling of the plane. But on the very last landing at La Guardia National Airport, there was a different response from the king. The runway there was bumpy with many holes and rough spots. Unexpectedly, the plane hit one of the holes, bounced, hit another one and bounced again. When they finally stopped, the king tapped Henry on the shoulder and said, "Captain—that was a real *stinker*."

Quoting from the book, *The Flying White House*, by J.F. ter Horst and Col. Ralph Albertazzie:

> President Roosevelt was the first Chief Executive to travel by air, the first to fly abroad, the first to visit a battle theater since Abraham Lincoln and the first to set foot on the continent of Africa. He achieved these distinctions in January 1943 when he flew on the Dixie Clipper from Miami to Casablanca in North Africa to meet with Prime Minister Churchill and Allied military leaders to plan the invasion of southern Europe. That trip accomplished one other thing of importance to the presidency and the future of aviation. It gave birth to the idea that there ought to be at least one airplane with the specific and primary

Major Myers Makes Record Over Water

MAJOR HENRY TIFT MYERS

Tifton, Ga, Sept. 23–Maj. Henry Tift Myers of Tifton is the first man to fly a plane around the world at or near the equator it became known here today in a letter just received by his mother, Mrs. Pearl Willingham Myers of Tifton. Also Maj. Myers is the first to fly a land plane from Ceylon to Australia, a distance of 3200 miles over water. Experts had previously considered this feat as an impossibility but Myers believed he could do it and accomplished it. The time was 15 1/2 hours.

Henry Tift Myers in the Cockpit

mission of transporting a president of the United States.

When President Roosevelt's trip to the Casablanca Conference was planned, Henry hoped to fly him on the *Guess Where II*. His hopes were dashed at the last minute because security had heard about the remote possibility of a malfunction in the C-87. Henry and his crew would fly to the Casablanca, Cairo, and Tehran Conferences as back-up in case they were needed. These conferences were held in a vacuum of silence. This was the agreed-upon procedure. But without letting the British or Americans know their intentions, the moment Stalin was back in Moscow the Russians broke the news of the meetings. At four in the morning, Press Secretary Steve Early called Henry and told him "Hell had busted wide open." Every paper, magazine, and radio station in the United States was screaming for facts about the conferences. "We've got to fly news and pictures to Washington," he told Henry. "How soon can you get there?" At the time there were two ferry routes across the Atlantic from Cairo—the tedious northern route, somewhat uncertain in December, and the southern route of which Henry said, "You fly for two days and land in Brazil—still further away from New York than when you started." To try and meet the deadline Henry decided to try a new route via the Azores, thereby

saving four thousand miles. This would cut about two days from the previous flying time. Permission to land in these Portuguese- owned islands would have to be negotiated—Portugal was neutral at the time. Henry knew that the British were operating an anti-submarine patrol base from one of the islands and if he could slip in there and land, he could make it. He told Steve Early, "Let me fly whatever route I decide on and your stuff will be in Washington thirty-six hours after we clear Cairo." A young courier arrived at the Cairo airport with a truckload of news material and Henry radioed a message to the British at Gibraltar requesting permission to land at their base in the Azores. Without waiting for an answer, he took off in the direction of Marrakech. Flying low on the water, the Azores finally came into view, but the British had not been advised of their flight plan. They radioed the C-87 and told it to go back. After going back and forth with the British, they finally agreed to let Henry land. The C-87 needed four thousand feet for landing and the field had only three thousand feet of landing space. The British radioed back: "Keep circling, we'll fill in the ditch."

Once on the ground on the Azores, the British came out in force to welcome the first American aircraft into the Azores. After twenty-one hours of flying time, another record and another new route had been

Hank Myers, pilot seat; Elmer Smith, co-pilot; Ted Boselli, navigator; Charles A. Horton (left), radio operator and R.W. Robitaille, steward master. U.S. Army A.A.F. photo.

The State Room of the *Sacred Cow* reflects FDR's love of the sea. The ship painting by Duncan Gleason was a gift to FDR from Donald Douglas.

FDR's wheelchair in the elevator of the *Sacred Cow*. ACME photo, June 4, 1945.

established. Later that day in Washington D.C., the first news accounts of the Tehran Conference were in print.

It became apparent that President Roosevelt needed his own specially equipped aircraft and plans were underway at the Douglas Aircraft Company to build a new C-54 with an elevator for the handicapped president. It was common knowledge and therefore a security nightmare, when the president would be arriving because of the thirty-foot ramps that had to be built a week before his arrival. In an interview after the war, Henry said: "There were a couple of instances where you saw the security was shot all to hell; there wasn't any secret situation about the thing, just on account of those ramps."

He also related that President Roosevelt much preferred to travel by sea or land because he could get more rest. With air travel, he arrived at his destination so quickly that there was not enough time for him to rest and get ready for the onslaught of the crowds and the press. However, it was necessary for the president to fly and General George said without hesitation that Henry Tift Myers would be the pilot. The following quotes are also from the book *The Flying Whitehouse*:

> While they outfitted an airplane especially

for the president, the generals were busy with another historic task—the selection of the first presidential pilot. Lt. Gen. Harold George, the three star boss of the Air Transport Command, personally made the choice. He assigned his own pilot, Maj. Henry Tift Myers, to the new position. "Hank" Myers was never much on military spit and polish. Myers coupled a soft drawl with flashing dark eyes and an infectious grin—the epitome of the dashing World War II "fly-boys" who flew like demons and broke women's hearts across the globe.

One thing that was known for sure is that Henry loved women—lots of them. To keep some of them happy, he would do a lot of shopping while in Europe, and his French lessons at the University of Georgia paid off. "We brought so much perfume back from France that we developed our own packaging system. Perfume is like a fountain pen. A fountain pen won't leak on the ground; you get it up in the air—most of them will leak. Well, perfume will, too, unless you set all the bottles straight up. The first time we did it, (brought back perfume) we lost a lot of perfume and the airplane smelled to high heaven," Henry recalled with a big grin.

By June, Henry had selected two men that he knew would be absolutely reliable for his presidential flight crew. They were Engineer M. Sgt. Fred A. Winslow and Radio Operator M. Sgt. Charles A. Horton. Later that summer, Henry took a senatorial committee on a tour of Alaska and that is where he found his new co-pilot, Capt. Elmer F. ("Smitty") Smith. Smitty was a handsome, blond young man from Clearwater, California, with an infectious smile, fresh out of flying school but without the cockiness that sometimes accompanied young pilots. Henry liked him immediately and the fact that Smitty had gained experience flying in the ice and snow of Alaska was a bonus.

Smitty, born on July 13, 1917, is the only original crewmember left. He resides in Sterling, Virginia, and this author and Henry's son, Tift, met with him, asking him to recall his experiences. Upon showing us his flight records, it was evident how painstakingly precise, accurate, and detailed they were. All of his photographs were neatly categorized, labeled, and protected from the elements. In contrast, Henry would write notes on the back of anything he could find and his multitude of photos were stuffed and packed in a thousand different places. Smitty's attention to detail, coupled with Henry's confidence and pure love of flying, made them a good match. "We were a good team," Smitty told us with his charming smile.

In August of 1943, Henry received the Distinguished Flying Cross for a 3,300-mile flight from Ceylon to Australia. This was a pioneering flight that skirted islands occupied by the Japanese. The navigator for this flight was Maj. Ted J. Boselli, a Greenville, South Carolina, athlete who had been with the famed 19th Bomber Group, which fought the Japanese all the way from the Philippines down to Australia. Boselli was Henry's navigator and the most-decorated member of the presidential crew.

By the time of the Cairo and Teheran Conferences, the selection of the crew of the presidential aircraft was complete with the addition of M. Sgt. Fred J. Willard, a tough and dependable Philadelphian with twenty-six years in the service and Steward M.

Left, Hank Myers and crew of the *Sacred Cow*. U.S. Army A.A.F. photo.

In 2004, Tift traveled to Virginia to meet his father's co-pilot, Elmer "Smitty" Smith; at 87 he is the only surviving crew member. Photo by the author.

Sgt. R. W. Robitaille, a Manhattan-born former Eastern Airlines steward.

The presidential airplane was built under such secrecy and confidentiality that no one was even allowed to mention it. Someone working in operations dubbed it the *Sacred Cow* and that became the code name for the aircraft. Hank further explains the name:

> Some way or another it got to Roosevelt that that was the name of the airplane. He mentioned it in talking to the press and the press picked it up and it has been named that ever since. There has been a lot of kick about the name *Sacred Cow*—people say that it's sacrilegious and what not. Like the other day, the Lutheran ministers were having a convention and complained about the name and suggested that the plane be called instead *The American Eagle* or *The Dove of Peace*—can you imagine me flying around in a plane called *The Dove of Peace?*

For weeks Henry stayed at the Douglas Aircraft Company in Santa Monica, California, in order to learn every detail about the new presidential plane. (The Douglas Aircraft Company was incorporated in 1921 and in 1967 the company merged with McDonall Aircraft, forming McDonall Douglas. In 1997, McDonall Douglas became a part of the Boeing Company.)

Donald Willis Douglas Sr., the founder and president of the Douglas Aircraft Company, had this to say about Henry:

> Hank Myers made valuable contributions to the development of the two presidential airplanes built by the Douglas Aircraft Company. Hank brought the rich background of experience as an ace pilot in airline operations and later as the man who had flown most of the world's celebrities across the seven seas and the principal continents. The engineers and the boys in the shop always welcomed Hank as a man who had something constructive to say about the job at hand.

In an *American Magazine* interview conducted by Jerome Beatty at the Raleigh Hotel in Washington, D.C., on September 18, 1946, Henry explained how the *Sacred Cow* came into being:

> At the Cairo Conference, people got scared of the C-87s (*The Guess Where II*). There had been some stories about them blowing up and the gas tanks did leak and it wasn't as good as the 54. So they decided they better haul him (Roosevelt) in the 54 again. They started building these ramps when we hit on the idea of building this plane with an elevator, the whole thing self-contained. Then we could take him out to the airport with no prior

This was one of the proposed insignia for the *Sacred Cow* designed by Edwin Todd.

The Sacred Cow

Walt Disney designed this insignia but the crew preferred the one at the top of this page.

The presidential phone onboard the *Sacred Cow*. ACME photo, June 4, 1945.

M. Sgt. R.W. Robitaille prepares a meal in the kitchen of the *Sacred Cow*.

preparation, load him in the elevator, take him where he was going and let him off.

We can carry twenty-five in it, but it will sleep six people and carry two Secret Service people who are not supposed to sleep anyhow. The airlines carry fifty passengers in the same type. It was originally designed for the airlines before the war. United, American, and Pan American put up the money with Douglas on a 50/50 basis to design this airplane for the first modern four-engine airplane. When the war came along, the Army took them all. Instead of building 100 or so, they built 1000. This one was pulled off the line, somewhere along the assembly line, and was then converted for this particular job.

When the reporter asked Henry how much the plane cost, he answered: "I wouldn't want to be quoted. I think it cost around a million bucks. American people being as they are, it is not a good idea to say."

The new plane was delivered in June of 1944, but there had to be a "shake down" to make sure everything was up to snuff. Logging seventy-five hours around the United States, Henry tried to duplicate conditions that he might later encounter. With minor adjustments, the plane was ready.

During an interview onboard the plane after the war was over, Henry told about the bulletproof windows on the *Sacred Cow*: "This whole panel on the ship will turn a 50-caliber bullet." When asked about weapons the crew carried on board he said, "We each carry a .45 and a couple of Carbines and, during the war, we carried two Browning automatic rifles just in case we got forced down out in the middle of the Sahara or somewhere."

The elevator on the *Sacred Cow* was cleverly hidden. Maj. Gen. Henry (Hap) Arnold used to bet other generals that they could not find the elevator—and they couldn't. When it was not in use, it could be folded up and completely hidden in the floor of the aircraft. "Everybody was scared of the damn elevator—was afraid that the thing would get started and go through the top of the airplane, so they put a lot of safety things on it," Henry once remembered. He also recalled that the day before they were going to pick up President Roosevelt, they decided to try the elevator to make sure it was working all right—and it did not work at all! "We only had about five hours before we had to put the Old Man on—we had electricians and everybody there. We found the only thing wrong was that it had too many safety things on it. After taking about half of the safety devices off, they got it to work."

When President Roosevelt first saw his new plane, he exclaimed "All the comforts of home!" The president wanted to do as much for himself as possible, so his stateroom was equipped with a panel of controls for lights, telephone and the radio: "It looked like a C-54 instrument panel," Henry said. There were maps on the wall and from his seat he could roll those maps down and look at them. The president could get himself to the bathroom with a little swivel chair and could have a conference in his stateroom for six people or so.

The elevator came in handy later when they carried Mrs. Martha Truman, the ninety-three year old mother of the new president. Also, during the war they carried a 300-pound cryptographic machine for deciphering codes. The machine was hard to grip and it was much easier to put it on the elevator. It was also used for Maj. Gen. Edwin M. Watson, President Roosevelt's friend, military aide, and secretary. On the return trip from Yalta to Cairo, the ailing Watson was loaded onto the *Sacred Cow* and then placed aboard a cruiser for home. He died at sea before reaching home. General Watson, known as Pa, (a name he earned as a cadet at West Point because of his knowledge and good judgment) was a classmate of George C. Patton and others of distinguished character. It was said that the press loved Pa Watson because of his great sense of humor and his practical jokes. He was married to Frances Nash, an heiress and a concert pianist known around the world. The general and Mrs. Watson had a beautiful, seventy-eight acre estate in Virginia called Kenwood, located a quarter mile past Jefferson's Monticello on land once owned by Jefferson. President Roosevelt's cousin, William A. Delano, designed their stately home. Later a guest cottage was added for President Roosevelt to use. Today the estate of General and Mrs. Watson is the home of the International Center for Jefferson Studies and also home to the Jefferson Library, which was bequeathed to the University of Virginia by Mrs. Watson.

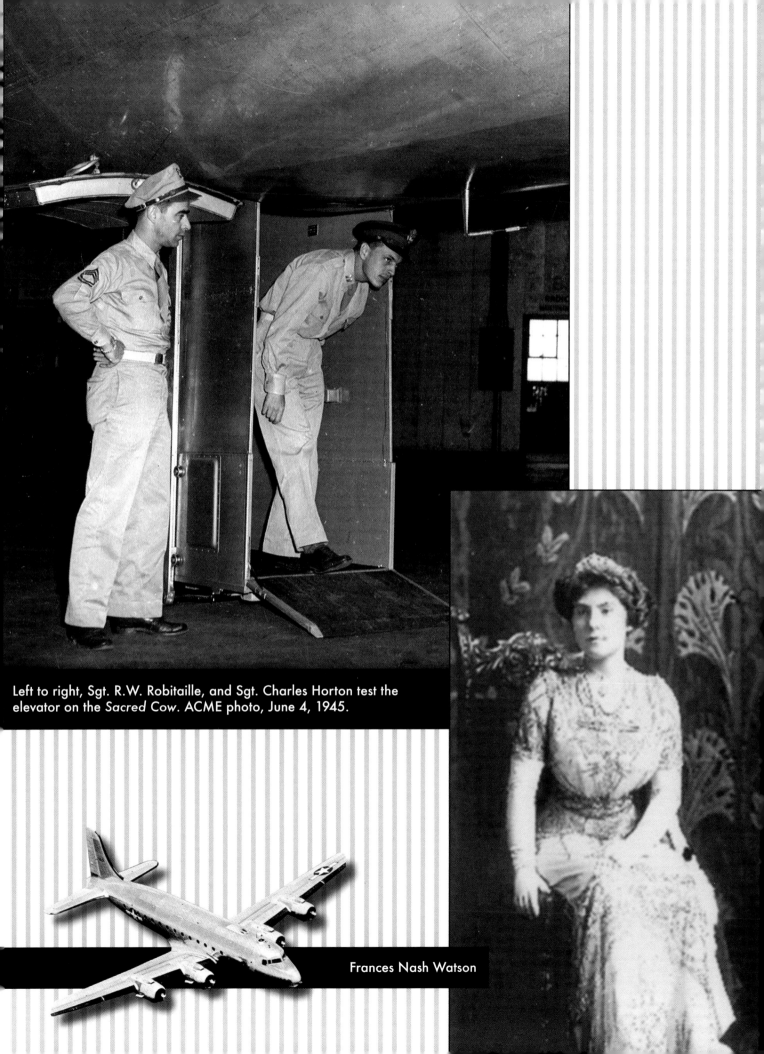

Left to right, Sgt. R.W. Robitaille, and Sgt. Charles Horton test the elevator on the *Sacred Cow*. ACME photo, June 4, 1945.

Frances Nash Watson

President Roosevelt lost his good friend and advisor on the return from Yalta on February 20, 1945. Six weeks later, the distressing news of Roosevelt's own death would be announced.

On a lighter note, in a letter to his mother dated August 17, 1944, Henry writes:

> Our trip was perfect in every way. That part of Alaska is wonderful this time of the year and of course I always enjoy Honolulu—got me a new girl there—this time with lots of money and the prettiest house on the island—so just moved in with her and enjoyed life thoroughly.

Pearl Myers, as mentioned earlier, was not as conventional in those times as her sisters. They would be horrified to read their nephew's letter. Henry and his mother shared a close relationship and she wanted him to enjoy what life had to offer.

Marguerite came home to Tifton every chance she could. This would eventually prove to be detrimental to her marriage to Roy. She had never had a *real* job before, other than helping her mother entertain at the Hotel Myon, something that they both thoroughly enjoyed doing. Now she was working with her husband in Maryland at Miller's Dutch Tavern—a far cry from what "Daddy's Girl" had been accustomed. Returning to Tifton, Marguerite would try to recapture her cherished memories of home and place. She and her brother Henry remained very close and would see each other as much as possible either in the Washington, D.C. area or when they both could come home to Tifton.

Pearl was spending more time at another one of her hotels, The Ocean View, and at her cottage on St. Simon's Island. In addition to these retreats, she had a cabin built on the lazy Alapaha River that operated as a fish camp. The fish camp, like her other properties, was operated so that guests felt welcomed and well fed. There was no shortage of accommodations for the Myers family reunions—just Henry's shortage of time.

Pearl loved both of her children equally, but she *liked* Henry the best. He was more like her—fearless, easygoing, and prudent with his spending. Marguerite's spending habits would have Pearl in an uproar and she constantly warned her daughter that she would be broke one day if she was not more careful.

Because Marguerite did not have children and was not interested in a career, her life began to revolve around church. Someone once said: "She was either comforting the afflicted or afflicting the comfortable," when it came to her religion. Although she was a staunch Baptist, Marguerite enjoyed making wine and having a beer or cocktail. She was not a hypocrite though, and did not try to hide the fact that she enjoyed a drink now and

69

Hank's girl in Hawaii tapes together his autographed currency to make a "short snorter".

Hank Myers "thoroughly enjoyed life" in Hawaii.

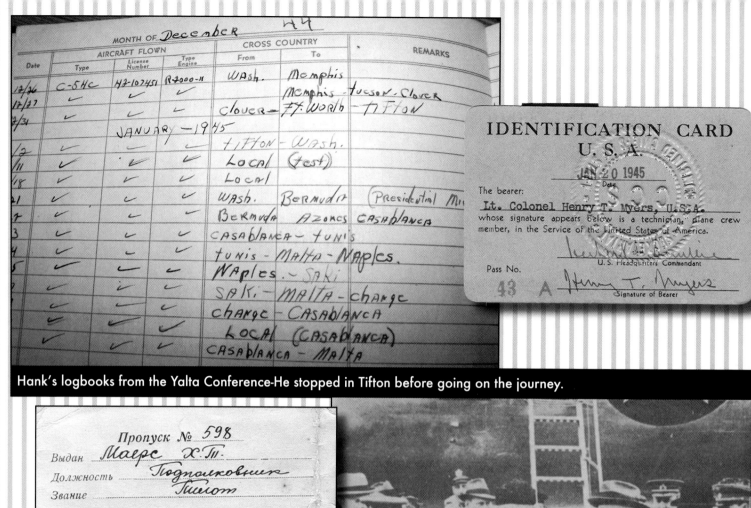

Hank's logbooks from the Yalta Conference-He stopped in Tifton before going on the journey.

A frail FDR leaves the *Sacred Cow* for the Yalta Conference as Winston Churchill puffs away on his cigar.

The *Sacred Cow* stands lonely in a Russian field. Its wings are covered to keep ice from forming.

then. Like her mother and brother, she was full of contradictions.

Henry's flight log entries are comical. The itineraries did not seem to fit—Paris, Washington, Cairo, New York, Washington, *Tifton*. When the *Sacred Cow* entered the South Georgia skies, Pearl would hop into her car and "fly" to the landing strip—her boy was home. It always caused quite a stir in the small Georgia town. *Air Force One* pilots of today probably are not allowed to take the Presidential plane home to see their mothers!

Flying with Winston Churchill was a trip in itself. Henry flew him from Quebec to Washington, D.C., on September 16, 1944. Soon after takeoff, Churchill appeared in the cockpit of the C-47 with a highball in one hand and a big, fresh cigar in the other, asking to be co-pilot. "I've flown many of these," he said; "in the RAF they are called Dakotas." Henry turned over the controls to Churchill who loosely grasped the wheel with one hand, keeping the other free to use for emphasis and animation to his unceasing conversation. Watching the compass and rate of climb indicator out of the corner of his eye, Henry noticed that one moment the nose of

the plane was in a 500-feet-a-minute climb, the next it was going down at the same rate. During a moment when Churchill was engaged in explaining to him an obscure bit of American history (the significance of the Tippacanoe River in nearby Ohio in the political life of President Benjamin Harrison), Henry switched the plane to automatic pilot. President Roosevelt met them at the airport and Churchill's words of greeting to him were: "Fortunately, I was along and could navigate the Dakota for your boys—otherwise we might have been late."

The first and only time that Henry flew President Roosevelt (FDR) was in February 1945 to the Yalta Conference. (Incidentally, FDR was the one who dubbed Henry, "Hank"—before then, he was always known as Henry or Brother.) Attending the Conference with FDR was his daughter Anna, who served as a caretaker to her ailing father as well as his secretary. Eleanor had wanted to go, but FDR thought that it would be better for Anna to go because both Churchill and Ambassador Harriman were taking their daughters. Anna was able to take care of her father without pestering him. "He might have been happier with a wife who was completely uncritical. That I was never able to be and he had to find it in other people," Eleanor said in her book, *This I Remember*.

Hank once made these observations about President Roosevelt:

The President was a pleasant, undemanding passenger and incidentally, a very fine navigator. At times, when I'd go back to tell him where we were, he'd already know. He'd follow our course on a map he kept before him. There was a time when we were flying through Turkey, pretty low, beneath the level of the mountain ranges and we were being careful to hit the right passes and so forth—well, we had to do a lot of circling around and I was sure the President wouldn't know where we were—but, by Lord! He had it plotted perfectly.

Before Hank actually flew the President to Yalta, he and the crew did a "dry run" to Yalta. Some of the nearby islands were still in nearby German hands. The Russian officials at Yalta showed Hank their charts and maps of the area and he later said, "Hell, we've got much better maps of Russia than Russia has." On that dry run to Yalta, other planes that were following him ran into a hail of "ack ack ack" so Hank knew which islands to avoid when flying FDR.

Also in attendance with FDR at the Yalta Conference were Adm. William D. Leahy, the chief of staff for FDR and later Truman; Fleet Adm. Earnest J. King; Gen. Paul Watson; Adm. Wilson Brown; Mike Reilly, who was the head of the White House Secret Service; Arthur Prettyman, the president's valet; and Harry Hopkins. "Harry the Hop," as FDR called him, lived in the White House and was the president's closest advisor—he was the man who persuaded the commander-in-chief to travel all the way to Yalta, even though he knew the president was ailing. It has now come to light that Harry Hopkins may actually have been a Soviet spy. Hank seemed to like Harry Hopkins and would probably be shocked to hear this news. In the 1990 book, *KGB: The Inside Story*, written in part by Oleg Gordievsky, a high level KGB defector, the damning information about Hopkins was reported. More information about Hopkin's

Accommodations in Yalta-the *Sacred Cow* crew decided to stay on the plane.

attling the cold, Hank and an unidentified friend pose under the ing of the *Sacred Cow*.

A Soviet guard ominously guards the airfield during the Yalta Conference.

Soviet official and Hank exchange pleasantries in the cold and arsh surroundings of the Yalta Conference.

connections with the Soviets was printed in *The Sword and the Shield: the Mitrokhin Archive.*

This book says that an agent identified as "19" reported a conversation between Roosevelt and Churchill and, "It is probable almost to the point of certainty that Hopkins was '19.'" (Historians seem to be split on the opinion that Hopkins was actually a Soviet spy.)

Hank had no interest in politics whatsoever and only had his mind on flying the President to his destination in Russia—not espionage. Because the President loved ships and it was thought to be safer for him at the time, FDR traveled first by ship to Malta. There he met with Prime Minister Churchill and then Hank flew him from Malta to Yalta. A U. S. squadron of fighters waiting in Greece escorted the Presidential aircraft as well as Churchill's airplane (code named *The Golden Bathtub*), which was following close behind. When they all arrived in Yalta, Churchill (who also had flown on a C-54) came aboard the *Sacred Cow* and looked around. Hank heard the Prime Minister say with some asperity under his breath something like, "Damn sight better looking than mine."

When the Yalta Conference was over, Hank flew President Roosevelt to Cairo and then the President boarded a cruiser for home. The crew of the *Cow* played "leapfrog" with President Roosevelt whenever he traveled. As mentioned earlier, the president preferred surface transportation, but he had to be able to fly if a crisis developed, so wherever he was, Hank and the crew were either right ahead of him or just behind him awaiting the call.

Something that Smitty remembered about the flight out of Yalta was that the fighter escorts somehow got their wires crossed and lost the presidential plane. "We are ahead of you," Smitty radioed to the fighter escort—they caught up with the *Cow* and were thoroughly humiliated. Hank never liked having an escort anyway because he thought it was not safe. According to him, sometimes the escort pilots would get too close to the presidential plane and try to wave at the VIPs on board.

Henry was the first person to fly nonstop to Paris after Lindberg. The crew took off from Washington, D.C., in the midst of increasing reports that the Allies were preparing for a winter of war on the Western Front. Among Hank's passengers on this historic flight were Gen. George C. Marshall, James F. Byrnes—then director of war-mobilization, and a small group of other high-ranking Army officials. Twenty hours later they landed at an airfield just outside of Paris and were met by General Eisenhower, Lt. Gen. Omar N. Bradley and Lt. Gen. Walter Bedell Smith.

Once, while Hank was in England with Secretary of War Henry Stimson, the call came from Washington to

While in Russia Hank took this picture of "The Big Three."

Harry Hopkins back to the camera, Secret Service Agent, Mike Reiley, (with handkerchief in pocket) and Hank to the right of Reiley, dine in a villa in Marrakech.

Unidentified Hollywood friend of Hank's.

Hank, unidentified woman and "Smitty" in England.
The Guess Where II is in the background.

The crew enjoys time off at an unknown beach.

Hank enjoys the beaches of South America.

come back home immediately. Hank made the eighteen hour, 3,800-mile hop nonstop, London to Washington, the first time it had ever been done.

On July 1, 1944, Hank flew the *Sacred Cow* on a vital mission, taking Secretary of War Stimson from Washington to Naples, Italy. His route was via Newfoundland, the Azores, and Casablanca, establishing another flying record. Secretary Stimson wrote Hank's boss, General George, and said:

> Major H. T. Myers and his entire crew were alert, attentive, and unusually capable in carrying out our duties. The entire crew should be commended for its high standard of flying efficiency. It was a great comfort to be able to sit back and relax, as soon as I boarded the plane, with so great a feeling of security.

They continued from Naples to Rome and in Hank's words "experienced the biggest celebration ever after Rome had been opened up." From Rome they took Secretary Stimson on to London. This was at the height of the VI bombings. Hank, always with his camera handy, snapped a picture from his London hotel moments after one of the bombs hit Hyde Park—you can almost feel the pandemonium when viewing the picture. On July 16, 1944, the *Sacred Cow* dropped the Secretary of War off at Normandy. "They just barely had a beachhead then. We just let him out and flew back to England and picked him up the next day," Hank remembered.

Early in 1944, when President Roosevelt went to Honolulu by cruiser and then on to Alaska, Hank played the leapfrog game with him and made the first nonstop flight from Honolulu to Alaska. By the time the president arrived in Alaska, the flight crew had found all of the good fishing places around Kodiak. Hank always carried his fishing tackle and shotgun on board—there was always a chance he could put them to use.

In dealing with so many top brass and their intermediaries, orders frequently got mixed up. Here, Hank explains one such episode:

> We took General Marshall into Paris about a week after Paris was liberated and there was still a lot of shooting going on in the streets and we were there when DeGaulle came up for his first

parade and everybody shot at him. I was right in front of the thing (parade) ducking. We had quite a time in Paris. (Shortly after this time, instructions were given to Hank by the brass to fly General Marshall back to Washington D.C.—they were to leave Paris at eleven p.m.) About eight o'clock, we arranged for transportation to go into the field. There was plenty of time to check on everything—and at just about eight o'clock it started raining. I never saw the rain fall so hard in my life. Of course, it was the darkest night—everything was blacked out. They sent the drivers around, with two cars; both of them were G.I. drivers on their first two days in Paris. The Paris streets are the darnedest things anyway. It takes an hour to get any place, so they were an hour late getting there, which made nine o'clock to start out to the field. We asked them to be sure to send us drivers that knew where Orly Field was located and they said they had been at Orly Field once, but not at night, but they thought they could find it. We drove about half an hour and nothing looked familiar to any of us and finally we made the drivers admit that they were lost. Here it was about ten o'clock and raining like hell and I was the only guy in the crowd who could speak French and I couldn't speak much French. I have practiced a lot more since then, but I could speak a little bit, so we would stop and ask a guy on the road where Orly Field was and hell, every one would start us off in a different direction and we would go around and around for a while, riding and then we would ask somebody else and they would send us back the other way, so it was really getting serious—finally, we stopped a gendarme of the French police and asked him and he started a rigmarole and I said, 'just get in the car with us, Bud,' so we put this French cop in too and we went to the field and we got there just in time to warm the engines up and get the airplane on the ramp before the general got there (General Marshall had been staying at the Palace of Versailles.) and somebody decided they ought to light the field to take off at night, so they turned out

Hank, the Eiffel Tower behind him, after Paris was liberated.

When the *Sacred* Cow landed in Paris, French girls were always on hand to help entertain the crew.

Hank and fellow Georgian Col. Bill Plummer of Atlanta in Paris after the liberation.

The *Sacred* Cow gets serviced at Orly Field in Paris.

all the kerosene lamps in the tents and so on and everybody around that whole area and they put them out there to light the field. As the airplane would go by, it would blow them out. We finally told them to give us a jeep to get us to the end of the runway and that was all we needed. The field had been heavily bombed and they just patched it up enough to get around. It was still raining to beat the band and we didn't run into anything except rain until we got to the English Channel. Going across the English Channel every ship challenged us and those surface vessels were really trigger-happy at that time. (It was necessary for Hank and his crew to identify their aircraft as American with the use of a signal pistol while crossing the channel.) The signal pistol mounts in this hole and you load the pistol and shoot it. It only takes thirty minutes to get across the channel at the widest point normally—we had to use every one of the cartridges before we got over.

When asked by the interviewer what General Marshall was doing during the flight, Hank said: "Nothing disturbs him anyway. In fact, I think we had the beds made down before he got on board and he went to bed and we flew across to St. Morgan, on Lands End and landed for gas and he was already asleep." (Orly Field in Paris did not have enough gasoline for a transatlantic flight.)

They finally landed in Washington, where it continued to rain. The flight took twenty-four hours and Hank said that they had to use instruments the whole way except for take-offs and landings. When they landed in Washington D.C., the general asked: "Why did we take off at night in the storm?"

"Why general, I understood you had ordered it that way," Hank answered.

"I didn't say anything about it—what would you have done if it had been left up to you?" General Marshall asked.

"I would have left in the afternoon," Hank told him.

"The next time you are flying me, do what you want to do," the general told Hank.

From that point on, Hank accepted no orders to fly unless they came from the mouth of the top brass and decisions to fly or not to fly were his judgment call. In Hank's view, General Marshall was the calmest, coolest passenger he ever carried and one of the kindest and most understanding, too.

During various other interviews, Hank was asked to remember the "close calls" that he and the crew encountered on the *Cow*. Some were rather humorous. Once they flew into a swarm of buzzards and another time there was an almost head-on collision in the mid-

Howard Hughes took Hank's ten-year air transport speed record held since 1934. Howard is fifth from the left and Hank is in the front with his hand in his pocket-Washington National Airport, April 21, 1944.

Left to right: Nelson Harvey, Roy Miller, and Marguerite at Miller's Dutch Tavern, 1947.

Fred Winslow feeds a hungry bear at a war-torn site.

While Hank and the crew were taxiing down the runway, a spitfire mistakenly opened fire and ripped their wing.

The Guess Where II, was a C87A 4 engine plane that was an adaptation of the B24 Liberator. Hank arrived at Karachi Air Base the evening of August 22, 1943 with five U.S. Senators on board.

Atlantic with what was probably the only other plane within a 500-mile radius! While in Paducah, Kentucky, with Senator Alben Barkley (later to be vice president under Truman), a large crowd gathered at the airport and at departure time, a crowd lined both sides of the runway to watch the great plane take off. There was a lot of excitement in the air and when Hank poured on the coal, a woman with five children clinging to her froze in the path of the plane. When it became apparent that they could not move out of the way, a split-second decision had to be made. Hank turned the plane, narrowly missing the woman and children. The wings of the aircraft skimmed over the heads of the crowd. Hank said that it was like making a turn in a car at forty miles per hour. Later, when things settled down, Hank kidded Senator Barkley by saying that his constituents in Kentucky were not very bright. Barkley's retort was quick: "Why man, my people aren't dumb—they just aren't afraid to die."

One of the most serious episodes on the *Cow* happened on July 13, 1946, while flying over the Irish Sea. When Smitty was asked about the lightning hitting the *Cow*, he remembered the incident as if it had happened yesterday. They were on their way from Paris back to Washington and had several furloughed GIs on board when they encountered severe weather over the Irish Sea. The lightning made a direct hit on the *Cow*. Without alarming the passengers, Hank made an unscheduled landing in Greenland so that he could check the plane for damage. Although visible holes dotted the fuselage of the aircraft, the *Cow* had escaped yet another threatening situation.

Smitty recalled an incident in 1943 that involved *Guess Where II*. It was after the Cairo Conference and they were leaving to go back to Washington D.C. Among the top brass on board was Secretary of the Treasury Henry Morgenthau. It seems that a British Spitfire, flown by a nervous pilot during an air raid alert, accidentally chewed up the wing of the *Guess Where II* while it was on the ground taxiing. The "cracker jack" crew of the *Guess Where II* stripped the whole wing panel off, replaced the wing and was ready to go home the next morning.

The craziest and most formidable flyers in the world, according to Hank, were the Russians: "They would not alter their path if another plane were heading toward them. They were downright fearless and liked to fly close to the ground, preferring to go around a cow rather than over it." Most of Russia is so flat that they didn't consider altitude that important. When Stalin's pilot was taking him from the Tehran Conference, he climbed to 12,000 feet to clear the Caucasus Mountains. Once he got over the mountains, he made a quick dive to get back down to where he was comfortable. Suddenly Stalin, already suffering from a head cold, had a burst eardrum. Hank didn't know what happened to the Russian pilot.

The trip to the Yalta Conference was filled with interesting incidents. The landing strip at Saki Airfield was very primitive. The *Sacred Cow* crew accommodations were in a building close to the landing strip. When Hank and the crew checked into their room, they discovered a microphone crudely hidden in the wall. Because the light in their room was too dim and they could not read, they spent the long evenings engaged in "make believe" conversation sure to give the spy network (NKVD) something to talk about! *Narodnyi komissariat vnutrennykh del*, or NKVD, was a powerful organization. In addition to controlling the police, it was in charge of border troops, fire brigades, convoy troops, and the entire penal system, which included regular prisons and forced labor camps. The Special Board attached to the NKVD operated outside the legal codes and could exile, deport, or confine to labor camps those persons deemed "socially dangerous."

The NKVD were ever present at the Yalta Conference. When Hank gave General Yermchenkov, head of the Russian Naval Air Force, some popular American magazines, they were quickly returned—the NKVD did not allow Soviet generals to be exposed to "bourgeois propaganda." While Hank was showing a Soviet newspaper-woman (who spoke English) around the plane, she saw a telephone beside a seat. Hank explained that almost every home in America had a phone. She was obviously impressed and started asking questions about American conveniences. A NKVD man in the group stopped her questions and elbowed her off the plane.

During a presentation in honor of her son, Pearl Myers reads a note from U.S. Sen. Walter F. George as Christy Bell Kennedy, Senator George's assistant, holds up Hank's portrait. Gen. C.R. Smith came as a proxy for Hank who was on a presidential mission.

Hank in full dress. U.S. Army A.A.F. photo.

Anna Roosevelt, as mentioned earlier, accompanied her father to the Yalta Conference. She and Hank drove to Sevastopol to inspect the damage done to the much fought over city. There were starving children everywhere. Anna and Hank started handing out candy bars to them. Immediately, NKVD men appeared and the children, said Hank, scattered "like frightened quail."

Bathing at the Soviet quarters seemed pretty impractical said Hank: "It is very difficult to enjoy a shower with women attendants running around and the showers were so arranged that when one person turned on the hot water, the shower next to him went cold and vice versa." When Smitty, Hank's co-pilot, was interviewed, he said with a big grin that what he remembered most about the Yalta Conference were the Russian women coming to get the crew and taking them to a large open shower, "like in gym class" and scrubbing each of them down. "There was a big cultural difference between us," Smitty said. After a few days of this, the crew moved back onto the plane. Hank got the Presidential Suite—probably the best accommodations at the Yalta Conference!

The Russians were proud of their autos, notably the Ziv. Hank was given one of the most frightening rides of his life by an enthusiastic Russian, anxious to demonstrate the Ziv's "superior" capabilities. Even though it was their latest model, Hank said that it was "a cross between a 1935 Buick and an Oakland." Its equipment was obsolete, but the Russian drove it like a demon on the winding roads from Yalta to Saki. "It was like taking a trans-Atlantic flight in a Model T. I was very happy to be safe on the *Cow* again," Hank recalled.

The food situation at the Yalta Conference left a lot to be desired. Although there were supply shortages, the Russians tried to outdo themselves, serving what they thought the Americans liked. The Russian bill of fare consisted of steak and eggs at every meal along with their favorite dishes of caviar, a very strong-tasting fish of some kind, hardtack (thick crackers), and the inevitable pitcher of vodka. Thinking that President Roosevelt might also be tiring of his diet, Hank volunteered to supplement his table. While on a special trip to Cairo for supplies, Hank and Gen. Ben Giles accepted an invitation from King Farouk to go duck hunting on his estate. Hank said that the hunting area was a two thousand-acre rice field with ducks as "thick as flies around a sugar bowl." Being a nimrod in the American tradition, Hank did not think it was very sporting—he had three assistants hand him guns, while men thrashed about in the rice fields to keep the ducks flying. That night, Hank sent FDR the best of his bag from the hunt. The president later complained that he never received the bounty and it was later suspected that those ducks were cooked and dished

The hosts of Yalta have a ceremony in honor of their guests.

Left, Hank and a crewmember visit an airplane "graveyard" in North Africa. The Messersmit wing ended up in Hank's den in Fort Worth, Texas.

Gil and Alice Mason with Hank in California. Gil Mason was the designer of *The Sacred Cow, The Independence,* and *The Guess Where II.*

A silhouette kiss for an Island girl.

Madame Chiang and her party proved to be the most difficult of Hank's passengers.

Another country and another girl......

Hank enjoying the company of Hilda Kay at Club Bali in California, 1942.

up to Stalin.

Speaking of food, Hank once served dinner to friends at his Washington apartment. The menu included bananas from Tahiti, oranges from Africa, pineapple and avocado from Brazil and steak from the British West Indies—all fresh! This showed the distance he traveled in any given week. What a way to do your grocery shopping!

Continuing on the subject of food, Secretary of State James F. Byrnes brought two big watermelons onboard the *Cow* in South Carolina and said to Hank: "I have got these two watermelons. One is for the crew and one for us." The crew tore off to Paris with the secretary of state and forgot about the watermelons. They stayed one day in Paris and then went back to Washington so they could fly President Truman to Kansas City. The President went there to vote and Hank related the account:

> Everybody got all tangled up with the President voting and we never got around to eating lunch and so when we got on board we were all hungry. Then we though about the watermelons—

probably the most well traveled watermelons in the world. They had been about ten thousand miles—South Carolina, Paris, Washington, Kansas City and Washington. The boss (President Truman) ate two pieces and declared them quite good—that just goes to show you how fast things move nowadays.

The largest load of cargo ever carried by Hank was for the Prince Regent of Iraq. During the United Nations Conference in 1945, the State Department asked him and the crew to take the Prince Regent, "Sidi," and twenty-two of his entourage from New York to San Francisco. "I never saw so much baggage in my life," he recalled.

The Prince Regent of Iraq may have had the largest load to carry, but according to Hank, Madame Chiang and her group were the largest burden to carry. Madame Chiang (nee Mayling Soong), wife of Chiang Kai-shek, was born in Shanghai in March of 1897. Her father was a Methodist minister and businessman who spent some fifteen years in the United States, where he attended Vanderbilt University, receiving a certificate in theology.

When Mayling was eleven years old she lived in Macon, Georgia. Her sister was a student at Wesleyan College. Mayling was tutored by Wesleyan students and easily picked up the English language—with a Southern accent. In 1913, she entered Wellesley College in Boston, Massachusetts, where she majored in English Literature and minored in philosophy, graduating with highest honors. With her days of living in Georgia, one would think that she would have learned some of the southern graces for which our region is known. Her detractors said that she was arrogant and referred to her as the "Chinese Dragon Lady."

It all began on September 3, 1944. Hank and the crew flew to New York to meet with Madame Chiang's people in order to plan a trip down to Rio de Janeiro, Brazil. Madame Chiang was resting there and wanted to come back to the United States to receive medical treatment. According to sources, she had a case of hives. (Whatever the ailment, it must not have been too serious—she passed away on October 23, 2003 at the age of 106!) At 3 p.m., the appointed time, the crew arrived in New York. They had been invited to have dinner with the Chinese after they had made the flight plans. Madame Chiang's nephew, T. V. Soong, was in charge of arrangements. T.V.'s father was the Foreign Minister of China. Hank and the crew waited all afternoon at LaGuardia Field. No word or sight of T.V. or any of his staff. Finally, at 2 a.m., he showed up with no explanation or apology, giving orders left and right. Finally, everyone was loaded aboard the plane and they were on their way. They had not been in the air thirty minutes when the steward came up to the cockpit and said to Hank: "The guy back there wants to see the Captain. He is raising hell and wants to see you now." The following conversation transpired:

> So I went back. He says, 'Col., you are the Capt. of the ship aren't you?' I
> said I was. He says, 'I will have a hot water bottle.' I say—you will have
> a hot water bottle? 'Yes.' We have got everything on the airplane you can
> think of but we haven't got a hot water bottle. He says—'Very inefficient.'

Hank Myers, the pilot seat; Elmer Smith, co-pilot; Ted Boselli, navigator; Fred A. Winslow (left), engineer; and Charles A. Horton, radio operator. Richard B. Russell Collection, Richard B. Russell Library for Political Research and Studies, The University of Georgia Libraries.

Hank and crew make a stop in Kwajalein (South Central Pacific).

Hank snapped this while in Tahiti.

There would be more "amusement" in store for crew of the *Cow*. Continuing the account:

We had had a beautiful trip until we got about to the Amazon River. It was always raining down there. There wasn't anything else wrong, except that it was raining like hell. When we got into the rain it scared hell out of him (T.V. Soong). He came up to me mighty insulted and said, 'You said the weather was going to be good.' I said, 'You can't travel 3,200 miles without getting into a little rain.' He said, 'My sister got all the way from China without getting in any rain.' I said, 'She must be a better pilot than I was.'

Hank did not like this guy at all. "He was a little prick if there ever was one," Hank recalled. For the rest of the trip Hank and the crew referred to the irritating T.V. Soong as "Junior."

Junior would come up to Hank and hold out his hand. At first Hank thought that he wanted to shake hands. Later, he found out that he wanted Hank to put a cigarette in his hand! On the return trip from Rio de Janeiro back to New York, it was agreed and understood that they were to leave at 11 p.m., from a Navy field thirty miles outside of Rio and that there would be eight passengers and no more than eight hundred pounds of baggage. Here is Hank's rendition of what transpired:

At 2:30 in the morning here comes Madame Chiang along with two trucks full of baggage. There must have been five or six thousand pounds of baggage. I said to Junior—I can't take all that baggage. The airplane won't get out of here with that load. Junior says—weigh it. I said how am I going to weigh the baggage out here at the airport at 2:30 in the morning, 2,000 miles from anywhere? I know how much baggage weighs; it doesn't take two trucks to bring 800 pounds of baggage. Finally, after getting nowhere with him, I told him to pick out what things you can't do without and I will have the rest of the goods shipped on the next Air Transport Command flight. You know, if he had just said that he was sorry for all the trouble, it would have been all right. There were no apologies—just orders.

This return trip that Hank made with Madame Chiang and her group was a first in aviation history, Rio de Janeiro to New York City—five thousand miles. This is what Hank remembered about that historic flight:

We made it in 22 hours and 53 minutes. We just kept on going—we had a good tail wind and were so anxious to get rid of that bunch of Chinks. Do you remember that hurricane that hit the East Coast? Well, we found it that

Hank ready to board for adventure. Associated Press photo.

Young girls clean Hank's accommodations in Casablanca.

Time for romance.
Paris 1944

Hank (in t-shirt) changes tire for Mrs. Roosevelt while on tour in the Caribbean.

Mrs. Roosevelt

The First Lady's Calling Card

Mrs. Roosevelt, always with a kind and encouraging word for "our boys."

Hank snapped this picture of Mrs. Roosevelt (right) and her secretary, Malvina Thompson, as they are escorted back to the aircraft. Malvina was Eleanor's trusted assistant and friend for 25 years.

night—it hadn't been reported. We found it out of Florida. I pulled into that thing, ran around it and went over to the Florida coast. We reported it then which was the first report of it. When we landed in New York, Junior came up front and said: 'The Madame is very appreciative of the service you have given. What do you think you deserve?' 'Oh, nothing at all, Bud,' I said, 'we are glad to be of service and any time we can be of service again, let us know.' I had been fairly polite, because I didn't want to start an international incident, but next time I saw Harry Hopkins I told him about Junior. Mr. Hopkins had had his troubles with Madame Chiang at the White House and he told me: 'You should have given him a swift kick in the pants' and, I said: 'Now you tell me!'

A short time later, a request came down from the Chinese embassy to get the names of all the crew. The names were sent in, but nothing was ever heard from the embassy. When Smitty was asked about the episode with Madame Chiang, he said she had to have silk sheets on the aircraft and it was generally agreed that she and her following were rude and unappreciative. While she was in New York, Jim Maloney, who was head of the New York branch of the Secret Service, had the responsibility of guarding her. He told Hank that he would get calls at 2 o'clock in the morning—Madame wanted to see him right away and he thought that she was threatened or something. Jim got out of bed and had to tear down through the Waldorf Hotel and up to the suite to meet her or her maid at the door. She wanted to mail a letter: "All she had to do was walk down the hall and drop the letter in the slot, or have the maid do it," Hank said in relating Jim's Maloney's experience with Madame Chiang. Unfortunately, Hank formed the same low opinion of Chiang Kai-shek, Madame Chiang's husband. "He treated us as if we were stevedores," he recalled.

There was only one complaint about Mrs. Roosevelt as a passenger: "She never stopped working. She was out to see the armed forces in military bases and hospitals and that's all she did. Traveling unofficially, she was able to duck social invitations so we didn't have much relaxation but when you would see her with those boys

95

in the God-forsaken bases and hospitals, you'd think it was worth it—Hell, it was like their own mother visiting them." Smitty agreed with Hank's assessment of Eleanor. "She was a good gal," he said. During wartime, Hank and the crew took her on a tour of American bases in the West Indies and Central and South America. "We tried to follow her on foot when she visited with the GIs, but, she wore us out, as she did the generals who guided her. She probably was the most experienced airline passenger we ever carried. Most of the time she worked with her secretary in her compartment and never wanted anybody to bother about her. She traveled light and we had no baggage problems," said Hank. Once while traveling with her in Australia, General McArthur arranged for her to stay in the fine hotel. She asked where the crew was staying and was told that they were in a place near the airport. The first lady demanded that the crew be moved to her hotel or she would join them at theirs. The general quickly moved the crew to the exclusive hotel. "I guess she was just a do-gooder," Hank recalled.

Eleanor wrote a syndicated column for American newspapers called "My Day," that chronicled her tour visiting "our boys." Quoting one of her articles:

> As in every other place where groups of men were gathered, I gave them a short message from their commander–in-chief. After leaving the Red Cross Club we saw a group of fliers just before they took off –you wish them luck with a catch in your throat because you know that, for the 'first timer,' there are experiences ahead of which he scarcely dreams.

When her South American tour was over, Eleanor conveyed her appreciation to Hank and the crew by giving each of them a beautiful wooden bowl bearing a silver plate commemorating the flight. Hank always said that she was one of the most appreciative passengers he had ever flown.

Another passenger who showed his appreciation according to Hank was Bernard Baruch, Chairman of the War Industries Board: "We took Mr. Baruch to London during the war and as we approached England we heard the German radio announcing that he was on his way to London by airplane and that the Germans were going to shoot him down. Neither Mr. Baruch nor the crew worried, since we were far away from any danger from German airplanes, but, when we landed safely, Mr. Baruch gave me $350 and told me to throw a party for the crew. It was quite a party."

One of the more hazardous and exhausting missions that Hank and the crew had was taking five United States senators to every stage in the world where Americans were fighting. This inspection committee consisted of

Darwin, Australia, Members of crew and party of world circling, senatorial mission, flown by ATC. Left to right: M. Sgt. F.A. Winslow, Senator Brewster, Senator Meade, Maj. T.J. Boselli, Senator Russell, Maj. E.F. Smith, Lt. Col. H.T. Myers, Senator Lodge, Senator Chandler, and M. Sgt. C.A. Horton. (Ranks are given as of May '46)

Hank, Capt. Steve Leo, and Senator Russell deep in a discussion.

Australia, 1943. Sen. Richard B. Russell and Hank. Richard B. Russell Collection, Richard B. Russell Library for Political Research and Studies, The University of Georgia Libraries.

Senator Russell and a recovering soldier at 81st Station Hospital, Biserte, North Africa, August 15, 1943. Richard B. Russell Collection, Richard B. Russell Library for Political Research and Studies, The University of Georgia Libraries.

Senator Brewster, Senator Chandler and Hank clowning around in Algeria.

Senators Richard B. Russell of Georgia, Henry Cabot Lodge of Massachusetts, James M. Mead of New York, Albert B. Chandler of Kentucky, and Ralph O. Brewster of Maine. The chairman of the five man committee was Senator Russell and he was "one of the nicer passengers" according to Smitty. Hank had been in the SAE fraternity at the University of Georgia with Senator Russell's younger brothers, Fielding and Alexander. Senator Russell had also pledged SAE some ten years earlier at the University of Georgia—more than likely, he and Hank enjoyed recalling old college memories while on the trip.

In July of 1943, the senatorial tour was to leave from Washington, D.C., traveling more that 45,000 miles and making stops to the theaters of operations in Europe, North African, Asia, the Pacific, and points in between. "It is my hope that this committee will return from this trip fortified with firsthand knowledge of conditions abroad which will aid the Congress in legislating more intelligently on war measures, as well as in endeavoring to work out a lasting peace. It will be a grueling undertaking and I did not seek the appointment, but I shall do my best to see that our mission is fulfilled,"

Senator Russell wrote in a letter dated July 20, 1943.

Senator Russell often wrote his mother back home in Winder, Georgia, while on the world tour. Here is an excerpt from one such letter, dated, August 24, 1943:

Since writing you from Cairo, we have been traveling through a very historic country and I am enclosing a map which shows the route to Abadan and the general direction from there to Karachi. The map is marked with historical and Biblical points of interest and I think you will enjoy looking over it. There is certainly nothing to see from a plane except the desert and masses of rock. I do not believe that I noticed a single habitation until we were near Basra. We flew over the area between the Euphrates and Tigris Rivers where the Garden of Eden was supposed to have been located. There are palm trees in allocated areas but the country has deteriorated since Adam and Eve lived there. My own personal view is that someone made a mistake and that the Garden of Eden was really located on the other side of the world in Northeast Georgia. I have never encountered such fierce heat as that prevailing in Abadan and Basra. It was around 125 degrees and the wind blowing through an automobile felt like an open steel furnace. Our boys are certainly doing a magnificent job under great difficulties in this entire area. We are taking off soon for Chungking. This place was bombed heavy by the Japs yesterday, which was supposed to be the day of our arrival there. It was the first bombing in two years and many of the British and American officers here think the Japs were putting on a show for our benefit.

As mentioned earlier, this fact-finding mission was laced with danger. Another letter written by Senator Russell to his mother told of other close encounters they had with the enemy:

We had some interesting experiences at Bizerte. The first night we arrived there a ship in the outer harbor was torpedoed and beached not far below our quarters which were right on the water front. The next night we had an air raid alarm about 4:30 a.m. and I had an opportunity to see and hear the anti-aircraft guns in action as well as hearing the German and Italian planes. They were said to have been laying mines around the harbor entrance. On our way down to Cairo across the Mediterranean we saw a large merchant ship dead in the water, apparently torpedoed, with a cruiser circling around her dropping depth charges. About an hour later, some 200 miles away we flew over a large convoy, which was escorted by war vessels and planes. It was one of our longest hops, but it was not very dreary for in addition to these interesting sights we were keeping our eyes peeled for any possible German reconnaissance planes which might be operating from Crete.

Another flying record established on this trip with the senators was when Hank became the first person to pilot a plane from Ceylon to Australia. "It was an uneventful flight though it was tiresome to be cooped up in the plane with so many extra gas tanks, rubber boats and so forth," Senator Russell wrote to his mother on September 8, 1943. That was Hank's method—always prepared, especially when embarking on a

Hank sports a Fez while in North Africa.

Senators Chandler, Russell and Brewster share a laugh with their Chinese hosts.

Senators Chandler, Brewster, Mead, and Russell with Americans stationed in Tunisia, August 1943. Richard B. Russell Collection, Richard B. Russell Library for Political Research and Studies, The University of Georgia Libraries.

journey in unknown territory.

One problem that the crew had was collecting the senators when it was time for take off. They each wanted to spend time with the soldiers from their respective states. Those soldiers could vote! To solve the problem of the tardy bureaucrats, a whistle was used to round them up. When the whistle failed to hurry them to the plane, Hank found a taxi horn at a second-hand shop in England. The loud blast of the horn carried authority and the senators would scurry on back to the plane. There were no more delays and the exhausting around-the-world senatorial tour would finally end in September of 1943.

The Congressional Record of September 30, 1943, contains the full report of the tour around the world, given to Congress by Senator Henry Cabot Lodge. The report reads in part:

> From Southern India we made the jump to Australia, 3,200 miles in length, which was an adventure for us but a tremendous achievement for our crew. I wish to pay my tribute to them. The crew consisted of Maj. Henry Myers, the Capt., a wise, resourceful leader; his capable copilot, Lt. Elmer Smith; the phenomenally accurate navigator, Capt. T. J. Bocelli; the radio operator, Sgt. Charles Horton; and the engineer,

> Sgt. Frederick Winslow. They measured up to the highest standards of the military profession.

> I ask senators to reflect for a moment on the implications of such a flight, which was made so easily and so smoothly. Certainly, if it is so simple to make such flights in the year 1943, it should be easier to fly even greater distances in the near future. The situation has implications for the future security of our country, which no responsible American can ignore.

To commemorate the flight, the crew of seven each received a beautifully framed map marking all of the destinations they traveled with the senators. The hand-painted scenes placed around the map denote significant events on the tour. Smitty's map is proudly displayed in a prominent location in his home in Virginia and a picture of his framed piece is included in this book. (Tift hopes that he can locate his father's framed piece to add to his collection.)

When President Roosevelt died on April 12, 1945, Hank was in Europe flying Barney Baruch, chairman of the War Industries Board. While they were in London, John G. Winant, the American ambassador to Britain, called to tell them that the President had died. One thing that Hank remembered vividly was how very sad and upset the British people were at the news. "I was going down the street and I was never so impressed with every Englishman you would see; he would stop, with tears in his eyes, practically, and express sorrow at his death. He was loved more outside the United States, by far more than he was in the United States; just like we think Churchill is a great man over here and over there half of them hate his guts."

The president's son Elliott served as an army photo-reconnaissance pilot and also happened to be in London. Hank picked up Elliott and they headed back to Washington. When they landed, the train carrying the president's body was just about in North Carolina.

Senator Russell showed his appreciation with this photograph he gave Hank.

This framed document was given to each of the crew members in appreciation of their service for taking the senators around the world on their fact-finding mission. Courtesy of Elmer F. "Smitty" Smith.

Route that Hank flew the senators on the fact-finding mission. *The United States News Magazine, 1943.*

FINAL
APPROACH

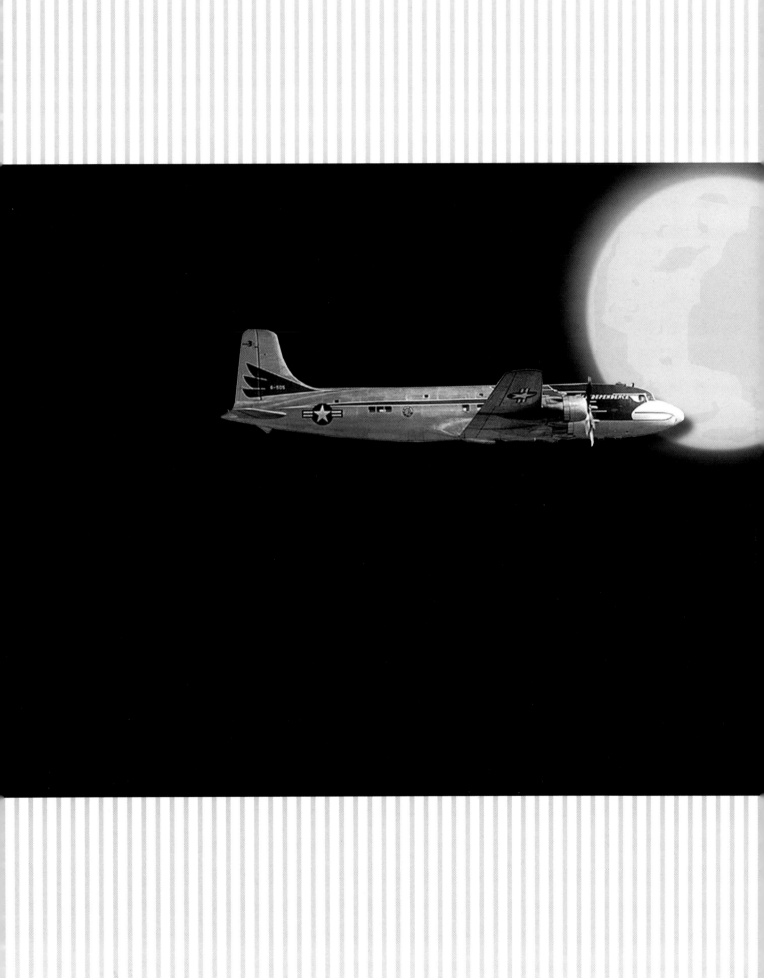

Harry Truman assumed the duty of commander in chief of the United States on April 12, 1945. On May 5, 1945, the *Sacred Cow* crew traveled to Kansas City, Missouri, to bring the new president's ninety-two year-old mother to Washington, D.C., for Mother's Day. The president's sister, Mary Jane, accompanied their mother, Martha, on the flight to Washington. This was the first time the ninety-two year old had ever flown and as the elevator of the *Sacred Cow* descended, the President, his daughter, Margaret, and press photographers with exploding flashbulbs rushed the matriarch. Wearing a new spring hat and a blue coat with a large purple orchid pinned on her shoulder; she made her way off the plane. "Oh, fiddle-sticks! If I had known this, I wouldn't have come," she muttered to her son, referring to the assembled press.

This new president loved to fly and unlike President Roosevelt, he preferred air travel to any other means of transportation. He was Hank's favorite passenger of all time. Inevitably, soon after take off Truman would appear at the cockpit ready to sit in the co-pilot's seat. This easy-going president enjoyed spending time with the crew, engaging in friendly repartee. He once said to Hank, "Don't fool with politics and I won't fool with flying." Hank was in no way interested in politics and the cockpit provided Truman with a secure place to vent his frustrations, knowing that the conversation

would stay right there. Truman loved just being one of the boys and according to Hank "he had a hard time remembering that he was someone important." Truman and the crew laughed, played poker, and told many a joke while onboard the presidential airplane.

Senator Alben Barkley, who would serve as Truman's vice president from 1949 until 1953, made the following observation about the new president in his book, *That Reminds Me*:

> When Truman succeeded to the presidency, he did so in a mood of extreme humility and some of his repeated statements about his 'unfitness' and 'inadequacy' for the job found their way to print. While I admired and respected this human quality in the man, I felt he was doing himself an injustice and that it was not good for the President of the United States to be quoted in such terms of self-deprecation. Finally I went to him-and there were others among his associates who did likewise-and spoke to him along these lines: Mr. President, I realize how you feel about this job that you have inherited and I respect you for your humility. But you have got the job and you have the responsibility. You are President of the United States and I hope you will no longer deprecate your own personal situation or minimize your ability to carry on the

Hank's favorite passenger of all time—Harry S. Truman.

This president loved to fly and promoted air travel whenever he could.

The president, his wife Bess, and daughter Margaret are all welcomed to Trinidad.

President Truman and daughter Margaret, at Sugarloaf Mountain in Brazil.

task to which you have been called. Gradually he grew more sure of himself and, commencing to act with vigor and assurance, he became a forceful and confident Chief Executive.

Because Hank and Harry were both from small, conservative parts of the country and, neither cared much for formality, they naturally got along very well. Harry's affable nature put everyone at ease. His 'regular guy' persona was in direct contrast to what the crew had experienced with President Roosevelt, who they found friendly and congenial but at the same time somewhat intimidating.

Smitty recalled that when President Truman traveled with Bess, she allowed him to have only one Scotch and soda. The President fixed that problem by making a visit to the cockpit where he could sneak another cocktail, safely away from the chastisement of his beloved Bess.

Unlike her husband, Mrs. Truman took no great pleasure in flying, but she was always a good sport. When she was attending the Inter American Defense Conference in Brazil with her husband, Hank told the president that he wanted to demonstrate the new reversible propellers on the aircraft. "I'm going to try them at Belem," he told President Truman. "Perhaps you ought to warn Mrs. Truman that they make a lot of noise." "No," said the president, "I'm not going to tell her anything. She's no baby." When they landed, the engines roared with a thunderous noise. Mrs. Truman asked her husband, "What caused that awful noise?" "The plane is falling apart," he said. "Well, if that's all that happens when it falls apart, it's all right with me," she bravely answered.

One thing that FDR and Truman did have in common was their love and knowledge of geography. While in the air, both of them plotted their location on the map and enjoyed finding out for themselves exactly where they were. Truman had learned to read maps as an artillery captain in World War 1 and Hank always said that Truman was a man of destiny because of his broad knowledge. The crew tried to stump him by asking obscure questions about America. One such question was: "Name the island that is home to the Statue of Liberty." Quick as a flash, President Truman answered, "Bedlow's Island." (The name was later changed to Liberty Island in 1956.)

As mentioned earlier, it was necessary for Hank to go to California to have the presidential aircraft serviced and the close proximity to Hollywood presented him the opportunity to meet actresses. One of the starlets that he dated was Audrey Trotter. She was in more than forty films during her career. One of the well-known films was *The Postman Always Rings Twice* starring Lana Turner. Audrey played the character Madge Gorland. Dorothy Kilgallen wrote a regular column called "The Voice of Broadway" for the *New York Journal-American*. In one of her articles she mentions Hank and Audrey: "Col. (sic) Henry Myers—the pilot who flew FDR to Yalta, Eisenhower back from Europe, and President Truman to San Francisco is skylarking with pretty Audrey Trotter between hops." President Truman saw the article in the paper and with a wink of his eye told his pilot: "Don't be seeing your girl on my time."

Years after this incident, Hank would again be in the company of a movie star. Arlene Dahl, the beautiful and popular actress from the 1950s, who later became a writer and businesswoman, came to Fort Worth in October of 1968. Hank escorted her all around town and again the event found its way into print.

Once, while in Brussels, Belgium, Hank had to tactfully ask Truman's secretary of state James Byrnes to get off the presidential plane. The secretary of the treasury, Henry Morgenthau, told Hank not to let the president and the secretary of state fly aboard the same plane because if something happened to both of them, he (Morgenthau) would become President of the United States—a job that he must not have wanted.

Most of Hank's passengers always observed a modicum of decorum but on a couple of occasions a group of minor officials climbed aboard the *Sacred Cow* loaded with enough alcohol for a trip to Mars. Their hilarity and carousing did not bother Hank but when some of the boozers tried to smoke in the mid-plane gasoline compartment, a very dangerous act, Hank decided that it was time for them to all go to sleep. He "dialed up" the altitude to 12,000 feet and stayed there until the thinner air combined

Laranjeiras Palace in Rio de Janeiro is where President Truman and his family stayed while in Brazil. Hank and the crew stayed in the beautiful Copacabana Palace Hotel.

The crew enjoying Rome, Italy.

On the back of this photograph Hank wrote: "Time off Paris"

with the alcohol gave his rowdy passengers the irresistible urge to snooze. The next day Hank explained the danger involved and asked that the next leg of the journey be made in comparitive sobriety. But when they arrived their pledges were forgotten and they were full of cheer for "Goo ol Hank." He poured them aboard, set the rate of climb indicator at 1,500 feet a minute and climbed for ten minutes and forty seconds. At 16,000 feet, with the crew sucking oxygen tubes, he leveled off and held it until he knew they were passed out and scheduled for tremendous hangovers. As long as they flew with Hank, this group never took another drink.

And then there was the nightime crossing of the Atlantic with Amir Saud, Crown Prince of Saudia Arabia, and his party. Suddenly Hank heard a tremendous thud on the floor on the cabin. At that moment, Steward Red Hughs burst through the compartment door and cried, "Hey, they're killing him." Hank rushed out to investigate. In the stateroom of the *Sacred Cow* four Saudi Arabians were tangled and piled up on the Prince whose smiling face beamed up from the floor. When they unraveled and all stood up, Hank learned that the free-for-all was an evening ritual and that the prince liked a little exercise before retiring, it made him sleep better. After the wrestling ordeal, the Saudi Arabians sang themselves to sleep. When they climbed into their berths there was a half hour of dissonant voices to be heard. "Finally only a single Arab

was left, a guy with a high voice. For a while I was afraid that he was an insomniac but eventually he got tired and ran down like an old bagpipe. After that it was so quiet over the Atlantic that you could hear a valve pop," Hank recalled.

During the heat of battle in the Philippines, Hank landed in Leyte with five generals who had a total of twelve stars between them. Here is how Hank related what happened next:

There was only one airstrip open at the time— Tacloban. When I landed, a Col. rushed up and said if we didn't get the plane off the strip in fifteen minutes they would shove it into the ocean. He meant it, too. The field held 200 planes; 230 were on it and a squadron of troop carriers, fifteen or more planes were coming in. I told the Col. we were the *Sacred Cow* and loaded with brass to see MacArthur and he said to me: There is a war going on here, bud. We don't need brass we need G.I.s. Off the strip or I'm sending a bulldozer to shove you off! So meekly I taxied the *Sacred Cow* to a take-off position at the end of the runway. As the plane neared the runway, sirens began to scream their red alert—Jap bombers were coming over. I saw the most amazing aircraft operations of my career—simultaneous landings and take-offs from opposite directions on the same strip. The

Actress Audrey Trotter and Hank dated while he was in the Hollywood vicinity. Truman saw an article about them in a California paper and told Hank with a wink in his eye, "Don't be seeing your girl on my time." Photo from www.Wikipedia.com.

Maps in the stateroom of the *Sacred Cow*—both FDR and Truman were excellent at pinpointing their exact location while flying.

The devastation at Potsdam, Germany, captured on film by Hank Myers.

Hank in Berlin during the Potsdam Conference.

Hank took this photo of his crew while in Potsdam for the conference.

troop carriers had to land at once; a squadron of radar equipped P-61s had to take off immediately to hunt the Japanese in the overcast and I had a grandstand seat. We were on the end of the runway facing the wind. At the other end a P-61 would start its run-down wind, with full power but holding onto the ground. Then a troop carrier C-47 would flash down over my head out of the rain, skim over the fighter and land just as the fighter pulled up into the air off the tip of my nose. By then another fighter had started its take-off. This split-second shuttlecock continued at thirty- second intervals until every plane had landed and every P-61 was airborne. It was the most perfect example of air teamwork I've ever seen.

On July 7, 1945, President Truman boarded the U.S.S. Augusta in Hampton Roads, Virginia. His final destination was Potsdam, Germany, where he met with the heads of government from the U.S.S.R. and the U.K. He arrived in Antwerp, Belgium, on July 15. He and his party traveled by car to an airfield in Brussels, Belgium. Hank and the crew then flew the president and his party to Berlin, with Potsdam only twenty-two miles away.

The Conference opened on July 17 and ended in the early morning hours of August 2. President Truman, Churchill, and Stalin met in the palace of the last crown prince of the German empire—the grand hall of the Cecilienhof. This was one of the few places that had not been damaged by the bombing. Never without his camera, Hank took many pictures of the devastation around Berlin and Potsdam.

The entries the president made in his diary during the conference make for fascinating reading. This conference presented Truman with heart-wrenching problems and decisions, including using the atomic bomb on Japan if they did not surrender. President Truman was anxious to get back home after this grueling meeting. Flying to Berlin, the president asked Hank about flying back to Washington rather than taking the ship. He was annoyed with how long the ocean voyage had taken. "We can leave at 5 o'clock in the afternoon and you'll be in Washington at about 9 a.m., the next morning," Hank told him. "You've talked me into it," Truman said. "I rest easy on a plane." But when the time came for the president to leave, the plans were changed. The president's advisors thought that the added security of the ship and the possibility for the president to get some rest would be better. "We flew him to Plymouth, England, where he met King George and then he returned by ship. I learned that it took terrific pressure to make him change his mind. He didn't give up until they got Mrs. Truman to telephone from Washington. When she put her foot down, he surrendered. Like most husbands, he knows who's boss." Hank said during an *American Magazine* interview.

A strange encounter happened before Hank left the Potsdam Conference. One of the wartime rumors was that ailing Stalin employed doubles at state or public functions. Hank saw the doubles. A paratrooper friend from Georgia named Bob Hall also happened to be in Berlin. He wanted to buy a Boxer pup to take home to Georgia. The best Boxer breeder lived in an apartment house deep in the Soviet Zone, Bob learned. Hank offered to get an interpreter and go with him to negotiate buying the pup. When they arrived, the breeder was most cordial—he had relatives in the United States. They all proceeded down to the basement of the apartment building where he kept the pups. Suddenly, a freight elevator door opened into the basement and out stepped three Tommy-gunned Russian guards. They looked around suspiciously and then motioned for the others on the elevator to follow them to an exit corridor. Out walked three men who looked exactly like the Joseph Stalin Hank had seen the day before at Potsdam. They were dressed in white pants with a wide gold stripe and an olive tunic with the insignia of a marshal. Through a tiny basement window Hank and his party watched the "triplets" enter a car waiting on the curb. Visibly shaken, the German dog breeder asked them to leave at once and would not even discuss the pup. Later when Hank recounted the incident to secret serviceman George Frescher, it was received without comment or surprise.

Henry and his future bride, Maidee Williams, kept in contact with each other during the trying war years. Not one to sit home and mope, Maidee continued to live life to the fullest in Fort Worth while she waited for Henry's return. She once got a job and excitedly rushed home to tell her father. He told her to quit immediately, that there

President Truman with the white hat and Hank, the second down from the president, on top of a captured German submarine. U.S. Navy photograph.

was someone else out there who needed that job. Maidee filled her days with bridge, tennis, parties, and travel. In retrospect, a job or career might have given her something to hang onto and a feeling of purpose later in her life.

Henry's logbooks reveal that he did come back to Fort Worth a good bit to see Maidee. Her father, Henry Williams, died in December of 1944 and the next year, Maidee would travel to Bethesda, Maryland, to marry her presidential pilot in a small ceremony at Marguerite's home—a new house that Pearl had bought for her daughter and son-in-law, Roy Miller.

For Henry's wedding gift, Pearl bought him a beautiful home on seventeen acres of land on Eagle Mountain Lake near Ft. Worth. Henry knew that he would return to Fort Worth and American Airlines after the war was over. The home was nestled far back off the road, offering peace and quiet. The lake was waiting just beyond his back door so he could easily take off in his boat when he had the notion. Henry would train his dogs to travel the quarter mile up the drive each morning to retrieve the newspaper. This would be the home Henry always returned to and loved for the rest of his life.

President Truman took the train to the Army-Navy game so that his pilot could have some time off, and on December 1, 1945, Hank came back to Washington long enough to get married. Washington would now be Maidee's home as long as Hank was the presidential pilot.

After a quick honeymoon in Mexico, Hank was off again. That first year of marriage was difficult for Maidee because her new husband was never there. Hank said that at one time early in their marriage "she was ready to pack it up and go home to Fort Worth."

Christmas of 1945 would not be a favorite holiday memory for the newlyweds. Not only could they not be together, Hank would receive unfair criticism from the press over the notorious Christmas Day flight of 1945. It seems that the president wanted to go home to Missouri to be with his family. Bess and Margaret left Washington the week before Christmas. Entries written in the president's diary reflect his somber mood at the time—he just wanted to go home. His health insurance plan was going nowhere; he was worried about the homeless vets, the picket lines, and labor problems. "Everybody wants something at the expense of everybody else and nobody thinks much of the other fellow," he wrote to his mother and sister.

Hank summed up the events of the flight this way:

> Mr. Truman wanted to leave at 8 a.m. on Christmas Day. For a couple of days I had been checking the weather and on Christmas Eve I telephoned Matt Connelly, one of the president's secretaries, that there was only a fifty-fifty chance that we could leave the next morning. He asked, 'what about getting out tonight?' That, I told

18

President Truman took the train to give Hank some time off so that he and Maidee could get married on December 1, 1945. Associated Press wire photo.

Off for a short honeymoon to Mexico. Maidee and Hank rarely saw each other their first year of marriage. Associated Press wire photo.

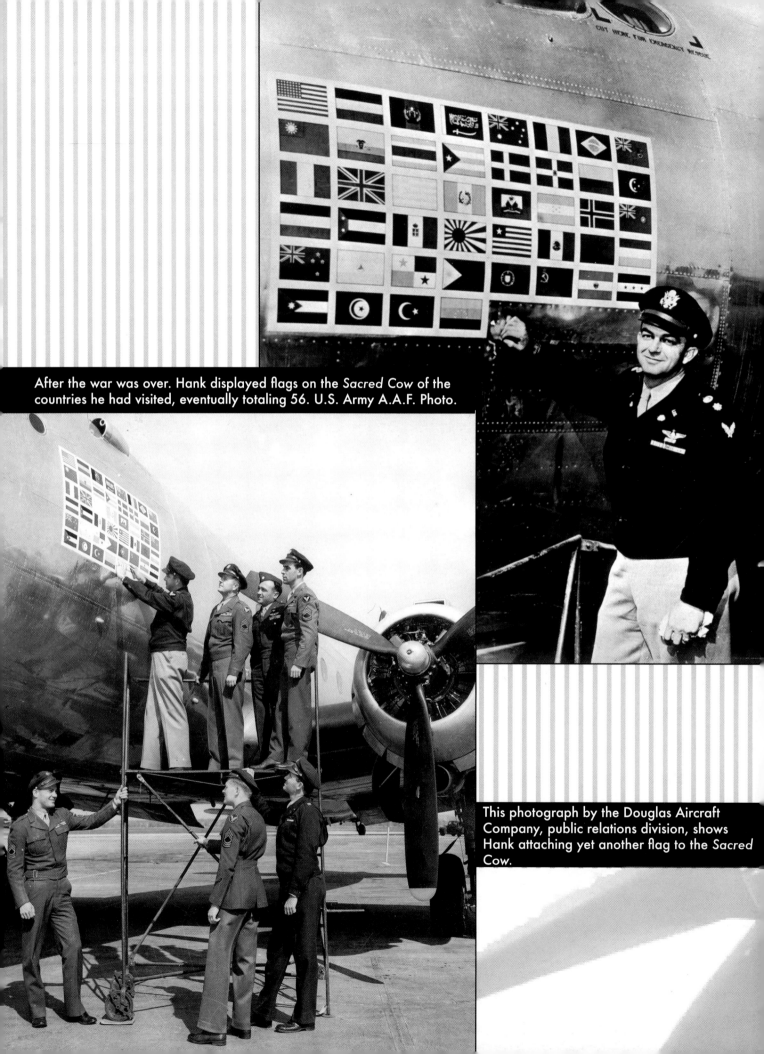

After the war was over. Hank displayed flags on the *Sacred Cow* of the countries he had visited, eventually totaling 56. U.S. Army A.A.F. Photo.

This photograph by the Douglas Aircraft Company, public relations division, shows Hank attaching yet another flag to the *Sacred Cow.*

him, 'was impossible.' The weather in Kansas City was too bad. The weather was flyable when I got to the field at 5 a.m. Christmas morning, but sleet started soon after, showing there was warm air aloft. You don't take off until you know how far you have to climb through ice to get into the warm air. I telephoned the White House, saying we couldn't leave at 8 o'clock, but to be ready for a call. In addition to other weather reports, we get "raob" reports. These are balloons that go up twenty thousand feet, broadcasting weather conditions as they go. Raob reported from Washington, Louisville, and St. Louis at 11 a.m., showing at what altitudes I could fly to keep out of ice. The temperature on the ground had gone up to 34 and the raob showed varying altitudes of non-freezing layers all the way to Indianapolis and other reports showed that if we approached a bad stretch we could pull south and go around by Nashville. This was the news we had been waiting for.

I notified the White House, Mr. Truman and his party arrived and we took off. It was a routine trip. We never changed our course. We dropped John W. Snyder and his family at St. Louis and went on to Kansas City. Now and then the trip was bumpy, but most of the time we were out in the clear. The president said it was a little rough, but that he had been on rougher trips. Nobody complained. I went to bed early at my hotel. About 8 a.m. the telephone started ringing so hard it almost jumped off the table. It was Gen. "Hap" Arnold, in Washington and he wanted to know what the hell had been going on. I didn't know what he was talking about. 'Haven't you seen the newspapers?' the general asked me. And when I said I hadn't, he said. 'Go down and get a paper and when you've read it, call me back.'

Big headlines told how the president had risked his life flying through pea soup and ice and into violent head winds that no commercial plane would dare. That was the beginning. For a week, news and editorial columns lambasted the president for making the trip and accused me of being the kind of pilot who would fly in a roaring blizzard just for the hell of it.

One reason for the wild stories was that the C-54 carrying eighteen reporters and photographers did have a bad trip. That plane had been brought out on the runway early in the morning and it became covered with ice. The *Cow* remained in the hangar. When the *Cow* left, they had to put the other airplane back in the hangar for two hours, to melt the sleet and when it got away the weather had changed for the worse. The reporters actually wrote about their own trip, not ours. They landed several hours behind us, plenty scared, for there was snow on the field blanketing the runways at Kansas City and their pilot never had landed there and had to make four or five passes at the field before he was able to land. The president laughed at the newspaper reports and he and his party flew back several days after Christmas. 'It's safer up here,' Truman said, than those icy Kansas City streets.' He was right. On the way back from the airport, the car that had brought him out skidded on the ice and crashed into a truck.

In the Truman Library there is a letter that the president wrote from Washington to his wife after the notorious Christmas Day flight. It seems that Bess had also given him hell about flying and it really hurt his feelings—he thought the she would be happy to see him and he needed comfort from the one he loved. After explaining his hurt to Bess, he signed the letter "I love you in season and out, Harry." Hank Myers had his own fences to mend with his new wife who did not enjoy spending their first Christmas apart.

You would have thought that Harry would have learned his lesson, but when the first P-80 jet fighters were brought to Washington to put on a demonstration, thousands of people, including Mrs. Truman and Margaret, went to their rooftops to watch. Hank was taking off with President Truman just as the P-80s came down to refuel. The president came up to the flight deck. "Do you suppose we could do a little something?" He asked. "Mrs. Truman and Margaret are on top of the White House. Couldn't we maybe—dive on them?" "Well it isn't dangerous, Mr. President,"

Maidee and Hank's first Christmas as newlyweds was overshadowed by Truman's infamous Christmas Day flight.

Roy Miller, Marguerite Myers Miller, Maidee, and Hank in Washington, D.C., Marguerite and "Brother" both lived in the D.C. area during the war years.

Maidee and Hank out for a stroll near their Washington, D.C. Apartment. 1946

Hank answered," but somebody will sure catch hell."
"I have wide shoulders," answered the president. They
climbed three thousand feet, circled the Whitehouse,
pushed the throttles and roared downward. Leveling off
at five hundred feet, the White House was as thoroughly
bussed as any building has ever been. Mrs. Truman and
Margaret waved. The president waved back at them and
beamed. "I guess we did all right for ourselves," said
President Truman. Later Jim Rowley, presidential secret
service, told Hank that the buzzing had given him an
efficiency check on his staff. "Every one of them turned
in the plane's number," he said proudly. Luckily, the press
did not have a field day with this caper.

Now that Hank was supposedly "off the market," his
former contacts would slowly learn about his marital
status. Maidee once told her friends that women would
often call their apartment in Washington, D.C., after
they were first married and ask to speak to Hank. They
were none too pleased when she said that "Mrs. Hank"
would be happy to deliver a message.

Another interest that Hank enjoyed was music and
he always kept an excellent record collection. He
once wrote a song after a trip to Tahiti that he named
"Tahitian Moon." When he took it to a singer that he
knew, she would not record it when she learned that he
was married!

Scribbled at the top of one of Hank's notebooks were
these words: "The two hardest jobs are interviews and
radio broadcasts. The most dangerous part of flying
is the wives' shopping service." He never enjoyed
interviews and was absolutely petrified when asked to do
live radio broadcast. As for the shopping service, Hank
was tightfisted, unless it was something that he really
wanted.

During these years, Pearl continued to operate the
Hotel Myon, The Ocean View Hotel, and manage the
farm, as well as rent out her tobacco warehouses. She
enjoyed entertaining the tobacco buyers and would pull
into the warehouse honking her car horn just as the
buyers were approaching her row of tobacco, bringing
the sale to a halt. Then she would proceed to serve
them ice-cold buttermilk—she always got top price for
her tobacco. Around this time, there was yet another
accident report involving Pearl. When the poor fellow
involved (a black man) hit the steering wheel and had his
teeth knocked out, Pearl said to the officer: "What's that
'darkie' crying about?-I take my teeth out every night."

In 1947 when Maidee learned that she was expecting a
baby, she moved back home to Fort Worth, Texas, so that
she could be taken care of by family and friends. Henry
Tift Myers, Jr. (Tift), was born on April 28, 1947, at
Harris Hospital. Hank would not be there for the arrival

124

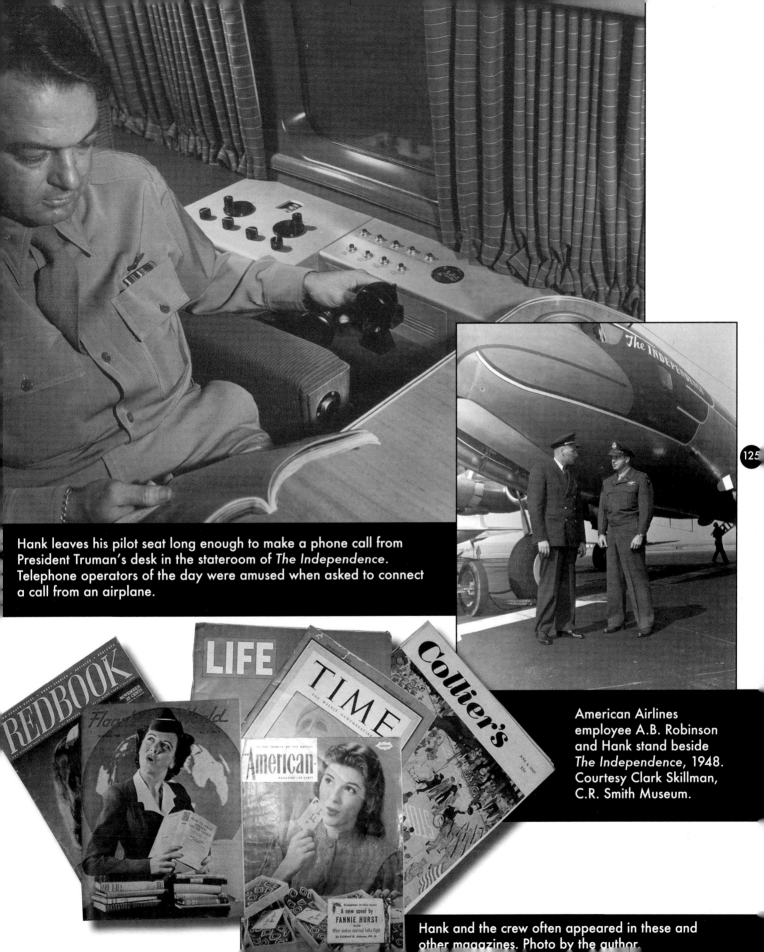

Hank leaves his pilot seat long enough to make a phone call from President Truman's desk in the stateroom of *The Independence*. Telephone operators of the day were amused when asked to connect a call from an airplane.

American Airlines employee A.B. Robinson and Hank stand beside *The Independence*, 1948. Courtesy Clark Skillman, C.R. Smith Museum.

Hank and the crew often appeared in these and other magazines. Photo by the author.

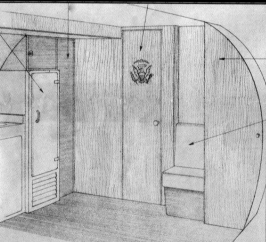

Henry T. Myers, Jr.

Best wishes for a long and happy life to the son of a great pilot.

The President

Harry Truman

The gift card that accompanied the silver porringer that President Truman sent to Tift on the occasion of his birth, 1947.

Tift was 11 days old when he met his father; this picture was in every major newspaper in the country. Associated Press Photo.

Hank Myers assisted with the design of both the *Sacred Cow* and *The Independence*. Drawing by R. Phillips, July 1, 1946.

After picking up Gen. Eisenhower in Paris, Hank and the crew bring him to Washington, D.C., to meet with President Truman.

of his first and only child because he had flown down to Mexico City to get President Miguel Aleman to bring him to Washington for a meeting on April 29 with President Truman.

Tift was 11 days old when he got to meet his father. When the presidential pilot arrived home in Fort Worth, the press was there taking pictures of him holding his new son with Maidee by his side. President Truman sent Tift a silver porringer with "Henry T. Myers, Jr." engraved on one side and "From the President of the United States, Harry S. Truman" on the other side. The enclosed card read: "Wishing a long and happy life to the son a great pilot, Harry Truman." The family picture showed up on the front page of every major newspaper in the country. Because of his pioneering flights, Hank was considered somewhat like an astronaut and he received a lot of media interest because of his proximity to the president. There were articles in Time, Life, Colliers, American, and Redbook magazines, as well as countless newspapers about Hank and his crew. With all of this attention from the press, the crew received a lot of fan mail—even marriage proposals!

Because of his unique career, Hank participated and witnessed many exciting moments in history, such as flying General Eisenhower back from Europe for his triumphant return, the liberation of Paris and Rome, and the wedding ceremony of Queen Elizabeth, to name a few. None of these compared to the welcome celebration he witnessed as he brought President Aleman home to Mexico City after his U. S. tour. Hank explained: "It was a gala like no other. I have never witnessed a demonstration to equal, either in volume or fervor; the welcome the Mexicans gave their president. It was simply terrific! For example, to begin the celebrations, as the *Sacred Cow* hit the runway, a 21-gun salute was fired from an entire battery of 155 mm guns—it was a deafening display of fire-power." Once again, Hank had the opportunity to witness history being made when President Truman signed the National Security Act of 1947 while on board the *Sacred Cow*. This Act established the Air Force as an independent service and the *Sacred Cow* is now considered the birthplace of the U.S. Air Force.

It was right about this time that the new presidential aircraft was designed and created at the Douglas Plant. Quoting from the book *The Flying Whitehouse*: "With the war over, the pace of development in the air transport industry was breathtaking. New technology in engines, metals, navigational instrumentation, and airframe construction warranted White House attention. In some ways, the *Sacred Cow* was like an aging hoofer who knew all the steps in the routine, but younger dancers had more agility and fewer wrinkles."

The name for the new airplane, *Independence*, was suggested by Hank in honor of President Truman's hometown in Missouri. As he did when the *Sacred Cow* was constructed, Hank spent many hours with the designers at Douglas getting acquainted with the DC-6 and offering suggestions as needed. There were some perks to this part of his job. With the remaining pieces of blue and grey fabric used inside the plane, a suit was made for Maidee and the cabinet builders made him a replica of the plane's bleached mahogany beverage bar. Tift now has the bar in his home, a wonderful souvenir from his father's career.

Two months after the *Independence* was commissioned, in September of 1947, President and Mrs. Truman and daughter Margaret took their first flight aboard the new plane. Their destination was Rio de Janeiro for the Inter-American Defense Conference. By November of the same year, the plane was returned to the Douglas plant. There had been a fatal accident with a DC-6 and the government ordered all of them grounded for inspection. The *Independence* was grounded for six months to make absolutely sure that everything was working perfectly. The old *Cow* loyally stood by as backup until the newer plane could soar again with confidence.

Speaking of confidence, Hank had all the confidence in the world in airplanes, but he did not think much of submarines and did not care to be in one. President Truman, on the other hand, enjoyed the underwater adventure and once insisted that his pilot accompany him on a captured German Schnorkel sub. The Schnorkel could attain a depth almost twice that of U. S. submarines of that time. "As we went deeper the Navy called off the fathoms with ominous funeral regularity. It sounded like a bell tolling for me," Hank said recalling the unpleasant memory. At a certain point while descending the depths, President Truman had arranged for a sailor to throw a bucket of water on

Hank and co-pilot Elmer F. Smith. Life Magazine photo by Peter Stackpole, 1947.

This stationery was provided on board the presidential aircraft. Hank gave it to friends as a souvenir when he visited Tifton in the presidential aircraft. Courtesy of R. Donald Dorminey.

We were terrified, and Truman was doubled up with laughter.

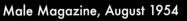

Male Magazine, August 1954

Hank and Harry in Key West.

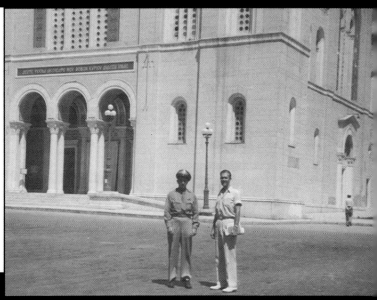

George Polk, a CBS radio reporter, and Hank in Athens, Greece, three days before Polk was murdered, 1948.

Hank. The president thought that it was very funny and Hank probably thought it was hilarious too, once he was back on terra ferma! While in Key West, Hank ended up being the envy of the Navy as he toured the submarine base on a powered bicycle he had picked up in Paris when he flew former Secretary of State Byrnes to a Foreign Minister's conference.

President Truman trusted Hank's judgment explicitly when it came to flying. When a sleet storm developed while the president was getting an honorary degree at Baylor University in Waco, Texas, Hank warned him that a slight temperature drop would ground them. Watching the thermometer like a hawk, when it hit 33 degrees, Hank sent the president a final call. The president rose during someone's speech, apologized and said, "Hank Myers says if I'm not at the airfield in 15 minutes, he won't take me to Washington."

In May of 1948, Hank flew a delegation to Greece and happened to meet up with George Polk, a CBS radio correspondent whom he knew. George Polk was born in Fort Worth, Texas. He and Hank had the "Texas connection" and for a while Polk had been assigned to the Washington, D.C., bureau of the Herald Tribune where their paths crossed many times. One of Hank's crew members took a picture of the two friends standing together; and it was only three days later that George Polk

went missing and was later found dead. George Polk had been living in Greece and was committed to reporting the truth about the Greek civil war that was raging at the time. The Greek population had already been through so much devastation when the Nazis occupied their country and now they had to endure a civil war. When Truman convinced Congress in 1947 to provide a $300 million aid package to Greece, Polk reported that mafia-like individuals were siphoning the money from the U.S. His body washed ashore in Salonika Bay eight days after his last broadcast. His murder was never solved. The prestigious George Polk Award for Journalism is presented annually in his honor.

Later in 1948, Hank decided to leave his position as presidential pilot. He felt that it was time to go back to Fort Worth and American Airlines. He had been getting a lot of "encouragement" from Maidee. She was ready to settle down to a more normal life and Hank was looking forward to having more free time to relax and enjoy his interests in boating and collecting automobiles. Not one for government interference and bureaucracy, Hank missed the free spirited days of flying he experienced during the war. He knew in his heart that it was time to move on to the next chapter in his life. There was also increasing political pressure on Truman to hire a crew from Missouri, the home base of Trans World Airlines.

American Airlines flight attendants welcome Hank back on board as Captain. Circa 1949

A happy Maidee Myers holds her new son. Rhea-Engert Studio photo.

The President did not want another pilot and said so in a newspaper article: "I don't care if Hank Myers is a Republican, I want him as my pilot." However, Hank was set in his decision to leave his job as aerial chauffeur for the president and after careful consideration, he recommended his friend Frenchy Williams as his successor. Lt. Col. Francis Williams, a native of Alameda, California, was an Air Force officer and also had flown for American Airlines. "I think a hell of a lot of Mr. Truman. I didn't want to turn the job over to somebody I thought couldn't handle it, and I think Frenchy can. Very few pilots think anyone else can fly anyway," Hank commented in a newspaper article.

President Truman offered his friend and pilot a general's star if he would stay in Washington, D.C., as one of his advisors. Hank thanked the president for the offer of the general's star, but his mind was made up. "I don't want to go to pink teas and hold coats for old ladies, but if you ever need a booster in Texas, let me know," Hank said to his favorite passenger of all time. President Truman had done more to advance aviation than anyone. He enjoyed flying and promoted it whenever he could and Hank always appreciated that. In fact, Truman

took great interest in plane gadgetry and allowed Hank to use the presidential aircraft as a flying laboratory. Improvements Hank made in the radar, reverse propellers, and pressurization of the cabin were accepted and used by commercial airlines.

Entries written in President Truman's diary show the regard that he had for Hank:

> March 4, 1947—Perfect day. Land at 10:00 on the dot. My pilot never misses a schedule. On July 29, 1947, he writes: Landed in Washington at 4:16- called Bess from White House. She was worried because our new pilots couldn't make the 'old cow' run as fast as Lt. Col. Myers can.

While Hank and Maidee lived in Washington, D.C., they often had dinner with President and Mrs. Truman at the White House. According to Tift, they were honored by the hospitality of President and Mrs. Truman and treasured the wonderful memories.

Now back in Fort Worth and resuming his flying career as a captain with American Airlines, Hank was still away most of the time. Tift said that he does not remember that much about his father when he was a young child, but he knew one thing—he could "fix the moon." He took young Tift outside and showed him a half moon or quarter moon and told him that when he got back home again, the moon would be round. He said he was going to go way up high in his plane and "fix the moon." Tift believed that he could do this. He thought that his dad could do anything. When Tift's own children were small, he would tell them that he would fix the moon for them. The only difference was that he ascended the skies in a hot air balloon, not a presidential aircraft!

Two pictures included in this book are very telling about Tift's early childhood in Fort Worth. In one picture, Tift is on his father's boat crying his eyes out while his parents look on apparently distressed as if they do not know what to make of him. The other picture taken the same day has the domestic staff onboard the boat. The maid is holding Tift while her petrified husband, the butler, sits stone-like from pure fright as Hank raced down the lake at breakneck speed.

Living out on the lake, there were not many kids around for young Tift to play with, but he was fortunate enough to have Ben. Ben lived on the Myers' property at the lake and was the son of their domestic help. Ben, a few years older, was like a big brother to the curious Tift and protected him from harm when he could. "Ben is the first one I think about when I recall childhood memories. He was my best friend back then," Tift said.

Maidee always kept young Tift neat, clean, and dressed like he was going to a party and engaged a well-known Fort Worth photographer to chronicle his growing-up years. Life seemed to be rolling along rather well and she hoped it would be even better now that Hank was home and flying with American Airlines out of Fort Worth.

When Tift was five years old, he was playing outside around a brick barbecue pit when he fell and hit his head. It was not certain if he would live because the wound was so severe. A grateful Maidee and Hank brought their son home after an extended stay at a Fort Worth Hospital. A reinforcement plate had to be put in his skull. This prevented him from ever participating in contact sports and years later the injury kept him from military service during the height of the Vietnam War. Tift views the injury as one of

Tift with his father and later at Culver Military Academy (top right).

Terrified domestic staff ride with Tift as Hank speeds along Eagle Mountain Lake.

Tift wails while on the boat as his parents look on helplessly.

life's mixed blessings.

Around the time Tift turned six, he began to hear whispers of words that he had never heard before—affair, separation, divorce, and the like. That summer his mother took him to Hawaii and they stayed in the beautiful oceanfront home of Maidee's uncle, Pat Calloway, an executive with United Artist Film Company. Tift didn't think much about his dad not being with them that summer—he was hardly ever around anyway. When they returned to Fort Worth in the fall for Tift to begin the first grade, his mother told him that they would be living in town and that she and his dad were getting a divorce. Hank Myers had been having an affair with an American Airlines flight attendant and it had reached a pinnacle. Maidee and everyone else (even Marguerite) found out about the affair. The marriage between the dashing pilot and the lovely Texas debutante was over.

Looking back, Tift thought that his dad's constant absences and his eye for the women, coupled with his mother's love of Scotch, strained their marriage. In his mother's defense, he said that it would be difficult for any woman to be married to his dad. "Hank Myers, along with his good qualities, was spoiled and selfish, but I don't think that he set out to hurt anyone—it just happened," Tift mused about his parents divorce.

Early after the divorce, Hank decided that he would not remarry. "I don't want to disappoint another woman,"

he once told Tift. However, there was always a special lady (or two or three) in his life. He was warm, witty, charming, and attentive to the ladies. He knew how to charm and wheedle the women. To this day, Tift says that he uses some of the same endearing terms with women that he heard his father use—but he laughingly says, "I don't think I have quite the same effect on the ladies!"

Hank's calm and easy going nature was in direct contrast to his love of speed and excitement in the air, the water, and on the road. He loved anything that had a motor—the faster the better. Hank was always responsible though—Tift saw him tipsy only once. It was during his retirement/sixtieth birthday party—"I guess that he had earned the right to cut loose and enjoy himself," Tift said.

After the divorce, Hank stayed at the home on Eagle Mountain Lake because it had been a gift to him from his mother. The house was sometimes referred to as the Myers' Museum. Among Hank's many souvenirs were a cuckoo clock and a radio that came out of Hitler's home in Berchesgarten, Germany. Also displayed in his home was a gold embossed swastika that came from the Chancellory in Berlin, a sandalwood perfume vial from Eva Braun's suicide chamber, a jeweled lighter initialed by the prince regent of Iraq, a pen with the engraved signature of the prime minister of Poland, an ivory-handled dagger that was a gift from Haile Selassie, and a thirty-five foot roll of "short snorters" bearing the signatures of Winston Churchill,

While his dad is "fixing the moon," Tift tries to fix his tricycle.

Maidee and her uncle, Pat Calloway. She and Tift stayed at his home in Hawaii the summer she left Hank.

Maryland Club Coffee

Mrs. Henry Myers, the former Maidee Williams. Active in the Barnaby Club, Fort Worth Garden Club, Cerebral Palsy Center. This petaled white organdy top, belted in red velvet over navy organza, fits into Mrs. Myers' busy calendar of informal summer evenings. By Ann Verdi, at The Fair.

Mrs. Myers' coffee . . . Maryland Club. First choice of those who want only the best! Full-bodied richness, deep winey flavor! Yes, here is the best . . . the very best! Everyone can enjoy Maryland Club. Everyone can enjoy a flavor bonus per cup and an economy bonus per pound in this super coffee. Maryland Club costs only two to three cents more than less flavorful brands. Ask your grocer for Maryland Club. You may as well enjoy the best.

*Mrs. Henry Myers, of Fort Worth. The fifth of a fashion-portrait series commissioned by Maryland Club Coffee...Photographed by Hence Griffith...Featuring socially-prominent Fort Worth women.

Maidee models for a coffee advertisement. Fort Worth Star Telegram, July 12, 1951.

Hank at his home draped in his 35 foot "short snorter;" the swastika hand embroidered by the wife of one of Hitler's henchmen hung at the Chancellery in Berlin. *Colliers Magazine 1949*

Best wishes + kindest regards to my good pilot

3/14/7 from Harry Truman

Old acquaintances Hank and Ike shake hands at arrival in Denver, Colorado. Ike is on the campaign trail in June of 1952 and Hank was designated to fly his American Airlines charter flight. Courtesy of American Airlines, C.R. Smith Museum.

FDR, Stalin, Truman, Eisenhower, and four hundred or so other major and minor history makers. (A short snorter is paper money taped together end to end with a collection of signatures; it was a popular fad during World War II.) Stalin signed his name on a separate bill from the one where FDR and Churchill had signed—he did not want his signature below theirs. Also in the home was a vast international coin collection, rugs from Morocco and Algeria, coffee tables from Peru, hassocks from Egypt and Turkey, dud bombs used as door stops and a wing from a German Messerschmit aircraft that Hank grabbed to bring home soon after the Germans left Tunis, the capitol of Tunisia in North Africa. (Smitty recalled that the day after Hank confiscated the Messerschmit wing, a booby trap exploded near the same location and killed an American GI. The Germans were known for setting up bombs in and around their abandoned military equipment to kill, maim, and terrify their enemy.) Many other souvenirs were proudly displayed all around Hank's home, commemorating his wartime travels. It is interesting to note that, unlike today, Hank and the crew did not have to bother with customs and regulations— they were allowed to bring whatever they wanted back home duty free, no questions asked.

When Tift was seven years old, Maidee married again for the third time. It was to another Texas oilman. The flamboyant Mervin Otto (M.O.) Rife became Tift's stepfather. Life would never be the same for Tift or Maidee. Ms. Inman, the live-in nanny, would do most of the parenting from then on and Tift would see his father even more infrequently. When a visit to his father's home was arranged, Tift eagerly went, but there was always a girlfriend around competing for his father's attention. Once in a while, Hank would take Tift on the plane with him for short trips and Tift remembers getting to sit in the pilot's seat with his dad and helping him to "fly the plane." As Tift grew older, he took advantage of free airline passes and would travel to Boston or New York just to have lunch and then come back to Fort Worth.

Maidee and her new husband, M.O, traveled frequently, leaving Tift at home with the nanny. Once when returning from Cuba they were greeted with the news that Tift and some of his grammar school friends had burned down a neighbor's barn while playing with matches. Another match episode happened when Tift and some of his buddies got curious about the sprinkler

139

More of Hank's souvenirs—the perfume vial was from Eva Braun's suicide chamber. Photo by Ulric Meisel, Dallas, Texas.

GLOBAL GUEST

FDR and Churchill signed Hank's "short snorter" at the Yalta Conference. When Stalin was asked to sign his name he asked for another bill because he did not want his signature to appear below theirs. Photo by Ulric Meisel, Dallas, Texas

War souvenirs surround Hank and his family. *Collier's Magazine*, 1949.

The cuckoo clock in Hank's den is from Hitler's home in Berchesgarten. *Collier's Magazine*, 1949.

system up in the ceiling at the River Crest Country Club. They wanted to know if it really worked. Tift remembers that it worked—very well. After M.O. wrote a check for damages to the club, Maidee conferred with Hank on military schools for Tift. He was sent that summer to Hank's alma mater, Culver Military Academy. When Tift was not asked to return in the fall, he was sent to Schriner Military Institute in Kerrville, Texas. After staying there about one year, he was asked not to return. Suwannee Military Academy in Tennessee was his mother's next choice for Tift's schooling. It was more remote than Schriner and there were no girls in sight. During a school break, Tift visited his grandmother Pearl in Tifton and rather than returning to Tennessee for school, he changed the airline ticket for Dallas/Fort Worth. He went AWOL. There were never serious consequences for his misbehavior from his parents. His dad was doing the thing he loved most in life, flying and seeing beautiful women, and his mother was always occupied with M.O. and the constant drinking, partying, and craziness that went along with their lifestyle. As a last resort, it was decided that Tift would live with his Aunt Marguerite and his grandmother in Tifton to complete his junior and senior years of high school.

Tift's well meaning but interfering aunt had her nose in all of his affairs. For the first time in his life, he had to answer for his actions. This was the opposite extreme of what he had been used to. Although she tried, Marguerite went overboard. She did not know what to do with children. She was very strict and super-involved with her First Baptist Church—Tift was a lapsed Episcopalian. Even when they went to the cottage on St. Simons Island for a weekend, Marguerite insisted that Tift attend church with her. He can remember lying in bed at the cottage early on a Sunday morning, just dying to go to the bathroom, but knowing that the creaking of the floor would awaken Marguerite. So miserably he lay there, hoping that Marguerite would oversleep and it would be too late to go to church. Sometimes it worked and he did not have to go to church. Pearl did not think that one had to attend church to find their Lord and as she grew older, she opted for a radio version of church services.

According to Tift, Marguerite made unnecessary demands of him. For example, she insisted that he sleep with a lady's stocking on his head because she did not like his cowlick! It was very humiliating for Tift and so was the fact that he had to be home earlier than his dates. This was a very difficult time for Marguerite and Tift. Pearl did not get involved. She was getting older and besides that she knew better—Marguerite ruled supreme at their house.

There was a presence that Marguerite had—you knew she was in the room. She could be an intimidating figure, especially at Tifton's First Baptist Church. Every Sunday

Boats were also a favorite—the faster the better.

Beautiful girls and wonderful cars always surrounded Hank.

143

Hank and his date: out for a formal evening and looking fine.

Maidee and Hank come together for Tift's graduation from Tift County High in 1966.

With Pearl and Marguerite in Tifton, Tift gets plenty of attention.

Pearl loved to bake cakes for her friends; here she delivers one to the Tifton telephone operators, circa 1950. Brown Studio, Tifton.

"Birthday celebration for a lovely lady and for many years known as Tifton's most unforgettable character," read the caption from The Tifton Gazette on May 26, 1965. Pearl died later that year at the age of 88.

Marguerite and Pearl join Hank at the airport dedication in 1961.

Hank addresses the guests at the Henry Tift Myers airport dedication. When Pearl told him the airport was being named in his honor he quipped, "but mother, I'm not dead yet."

and "when the doors were open and sometimes, even when they weren't," she would be at church. Those unaware of her seating position were quickly told to move as she approached the left side of the pew, one-third of the way from the pulpit. Usually wearing a peculiar hat like Queen Elizabeth, she would make her way to her "throne."

Pearl Myers became known to her many friends in Tifton as "Aunt Pearl." The no-nonsense, no-frills woman was loved and admired by the community just as her husband Irvine had been. She was always baking a cake or doing something for someone. In 1963, a friend wrote these words that appeared in the *Tifton Gazette*:

Aunt Pearl, being one of the largest taxpayers in the city, would call up and ask that someone from city hall come by her house to pick up her check for her property taxes. (She was not able to drive then.) Always then, she would say, 'I have baked another cake which I want you to take to my darling, precious friends at City Hall.'

Tift's hardworking, energetic grandmother grew frail and near the end of her life was confined to a wheel chair. Visits from her son, Henry, were what she lived for. As long as anyone can remember, this framed piece

hung on a wall on the porch of Pearl's farmhouse—the same porch where she served gallons of ice cream, lemonade, watermelons, cakes, and cookies to family and friends. This little ditty summed up her philosophy of life and today it hangs in Tift's kitchen as a reminder of his beloved grandmother.

Pearl died in November of 1965 at the age of 88. Her tombstone simply reads "Priceless Pearl" and indeed she was. The morning of his grandmother's death, Tift heard Marguerite phone her former husband, Roy, in Maryland, to tell him that he did not have to send her any more alimony payments; she knew that she would be set for life.

Tift's parents were congenial enough after divorcing to fly to Tifton together for his high school graduation in

1966. Together they overruled Marguerite's objections and he was permitted to stay out past 11 p.m. on graduation night. After graduation, Tift stayed on with Marguerite and attended Abraham Baldwin Agricultural College. When he did not return home in time to escort Marguerite and her signature cheese biscuits to a church function, all hell broke loose. "Heck, I was getting help with algebra from a tutor—I had a good reason for being late but it didn't matter to her. She and I had words. That's when I decided it was time to go back to Texas and I did, that very night," he remembered.

Maidee and M.O. had two sons of their own—David Rife, born in 1956 and Mark Rife, born in 1958. Like Tift, his half brothers were sent away to school, but, unlike him, they loved it. Judson Boarding School, in Paradise Valley, Arizona, offered many more amenities than did the military schools Tift attended. Because they were separated by years and distance, Tift's half brothers always seemed more like friends than brothers. His flashy stepfather, M.O., and his mother lived a fast and volatile life. It was not a home conducive to family life. At their home, liquor and beer were brought in by the caseload. Tift had been drinking alcohol with no reprisal since he was 13 years old. M.O. loved to entertain his wildcat oil friends around the swimming pool at their large, contemporary home in Forth Worth. In the early 1960s, their home was featured in a national magazine because it had so many modern gadgets, like remote control draperies, a stereo system that would hold more than one hundred records at a time, and an intercom system throughout the house. All of the trappings didn't really matter to Tift—he had learned early on that just having money did not make for a happy home. As the drinking increased, so did the arguing between Maidee and M.O. and in 1965 Maidee filed for divorce. Three attempts at finding a happy marriage had failed. Maidee would not try again.

While attending a class at the University of Oklahoma in December of 1968, Tift received a call from Marguerite. She told him that his father had just passed away. Ironically, six years later, he would be attending a class when he received a call with the news that his mother had died. They had been expecting the news about his father.

Sharing a flying story with a friend as Tift looks on. Associated Press photo.

Replicas of The *Sacred Cow* and The *Independence*, compliments of the Douglas Aircraft Company, were among his favorite souvenirs. Fort Worth Star Telegram, circa October, 1967

American Airlines flight attendants "decorate" Hank's cake ceremony.

Mitzi Caulder, American Airlines flight attendant, Hank, and C.R. Smith, CEO of American Airlines with Hank's retirement cake.

Hank had been hospitalized because of arteriosclerosis with congestive heart failure—the same disease that took his father, Irvine, at the same age of sixty-one. American Airlines had grounded Hank just before his sixtieth birthday because of his heart condition. What he loved most in life was now a thing of the past. With his wings clipped, his purpose and reason for living had slipped away. Marguerite came out to Ft. Worth to plan a memorial service. The actual funeral and burial would be held in his hometown of Tifton. In Hank Myers' true fashion, one of his girlfriends provided her family's private plane to take his body back to Georgia and another girlfriend accompanied Tift and Marguerite onboard the plane. There was never a shortage of women in his life—or his death. They all loved Hank.

His estate in Fort Worth was settled by Marguerite. She sold his beautiful home at Eagle Mountain Lake. Tift was left with a trust fund from his father that Marguerite controlled. It was enough to live on. He was in good shape materially for a twenty-one year old. He had three cars, a dune buggy, a boat, an apartment, and friends who loved to party. Unlike his dad, who knew from a young age what he wanted to do with his life, Tift had not discovered his life's purpose and unfortunately he did not have a role model to emulate. He became a true pot-smoking child of the sixties, drifting along without direction or motivation, wearing peace-sign t-shirts, bell-bottom jeans and shoulder length hair.

Once, while Tift was in New York to see his friend from Fort Worth, Delbert McClinton, perform on *Saturday Night Live*, he ended up in a limousine with John Belushi and they partied all night around New York—wild times indeed for a kid from Fort Worth. Another musical friend of Tift's, Glen Clark, was the keyboard player for Kris Kristofferson. Tift once arranged for Glen and Kris, (both avid fishermen) to come to the Alapaha River after performing a concert in Georgia. They stayed in the cabin Pearl had built years earlier as her fish camp. They enjoyed the remote setting and the lazy river offered them a respite from their harried concert schedule.

In the early 1970s, Tift and a couple of his friends opened a restaurant and bar on fourteen acres of land in Austin, Texas. They called it *The Friend Factory*. By this time Tift was married to a Fort Worth girl named Teresa Sedberry and they had a daughter named Tiffany. Marguerite allowed for his trust fund from his father to be increased to support his family. Although he continued to enjoy drinking and partying, he soon found out that the business in Austin was not for him and he returned with his new family to Fort Worth. He attended North Texas State University, pursuing an interest in photography. He would later invest in oil wells with his half brothers, David and Mark. This business was fairly successful but again, Tift decided that it was not for him.

Left to right: Talia Myers, Glen Clark, Tiffany Myers, and Kris Kristofferson, circa 1980.
Photo by Henry Tift Myers, Jr.

Like his father, Tift loves boating. Here he is on Eagle Mountain Lake in his boat, *The Sudden Urge*, circa 1985.

Unlike his father, Tift found it difficult to find his niche—for a while, he tried the oil business.

Although imperfect vision prohibited Tift from obtaining his pilot's license, he often took to the sky in hot air balloons with his camera in tow. Photos by Henry Tift Myers, Jr.

Tift's second daughter, Talia, was born in 1974 but his marriage would not last and he and Teresa divorced in 1976. Thankfully though, something connected in him as a parent and he realized that his girls, Tiffany and Talia, were the most important part of his life. He knew what he had missed as a child and his strong and solid relationship with his daughters is, according to him, his greatest accomplishment.

After divorcing M.O., Maidee spent most of her time at the country club playing bridge. She also enjoyed the company of a dear friend from her girlhood days, Gordon Arnold. Sweet and lovely Maidee, Tift's mother, died in November of 1974. She was only fifty-seven years old. At the time of her death, Maidee was living in Monticello Park, a beautiful older section of Fort Worth. Tift inherited her home and operated a photography business from there. The park was a great place for portrait photography and he turned out to be quite good, having a creative eye, a pleasant disposition, and a friendly manner that put his patrons at ease. Along with photography, he developed an interest in hot air balloons. Tift had always wanted to fly a plane like his father but he could not get a pilot's license because he did not have perfect vision. Good friends of his were hot air balloon enthusiasts and they encouraged him to go along with them as part of the crew. They attended the Albuquerque Balloon Fiesta (the largest annual balloon meet in the world) as well as meets in Aspen, Steamboat Springs, Idaho, and Utah. His newfound hobby also interested his daughter, Talia, and she often went with him. Like his father, Tift had found something that he enjoyed—taking to the skies. "Moving along with the wind, it was totally silent up there—very peaceful and the view was breathtaking," Tift recalled.

Also like his father, many women were in and out of Tift's life on a regular basis, but he would not commit himself. He basically did what he pleased unless it involved his daughters. In that one area—as a parent—he was determined to be responsible and dedicated and somehow he was. He enjoyed attending events and school functions with his girls and taking pictures of their every achievement. They knew that their dad would always be there for them.

Marguerite and Tift were the last of the Myers

immediate family and they kept in close contact after they lost Pearl and Hank. Tift would try to appeal to his aunt's better nature by calling her Mom—she liked that. She could still be difficult, but he could handle it in small doses. One family friend likened Marguerite to a chestnut burr that had a jewel inside—prickly on the outside, but good deep down inside.

She and Tift once traveled to England and Scotland and had the most enjoyable time. At Marguerite's urging, Tift later took his daughter, Tiffany, to see the original Passion Play in Oberammergau, Germany—something that Marguerite had taken many to see before. It was a moving experience that Tift would always remember.

Marguerite, as mentioned earlier, had control of Tift's inheritance from his father. After Pearl died, Marguerite revoked her mother's will and made a new one, cutting Tift out of his inheritance from his grandmother. It didn't matter to Tift because all of the money had been given away by then and all of the property had been sold. Marguerite paid for educations, bought cars for people, took friends to Europe, and gave generously to Jim and Tammy Faye Baker, Oral Roberts, Billy Graham, orphans in India, missionaries in China, and always to her church. The once-sizable Myers estate had finally been exhausted. When she grew old and could no longer care for herself, she was moved to a nursing home. The once proud and wealthy woman died penniless at the age of ninety-two. It was just as Pearl had predicted when she frequently admonished her daughter: "Marguerite, you're going to die broke if you don't stop giving it all away."

The years passed, as they do, and Tift's daughters married and had their own children. When Tift was diagnosed with Type-1 diabetes and high blood pressure, he realized that he would have to make radical changes in his life. A seed was planted in his mind and during the next few years, the simple and wholesome life of the small town in Georgia began to beckon to him. His grandmother and Marguerite were gone but not the memories of time spent there. Finally, in 1999, he was resolute in his decision to move to Georgia and leave the fast-paced city life behind. It was difficult for him to leave his daughters and granddaughters in Fort Worth, but they understood and just wanted him

Tift arrives in Tifton for a visit with daughter Tiffany in tow.

Knowing how it felt to not have a father around, Tift spent as much time as possible with his daughters.

Ted, "Smitty," and Hank ride camels in Cairo, Egypt.

Tift rides a camel in Egypt like his father had done years before, circa 1985.

to get well at any cost.

After returning to Georgia, Tift was able to retrieve his father's collection of pictures, letters, and manuscripts from his flying career. His interest in his father's life was regenerated after his move to Tifton and he found that he enjoys speaking to groups and organizations about his father's unusual career. It seems that what Hank Myers feared and disliked the most (public speaking) is what Tift Myers just naturally enjoys. Tift has also taken great pleasure in learning about his family's early history in Georgia and feels a new connection with his extended family.

Yes, Lt. Col. Henry Tift Myers was a man just like any other, a universal man full of contradictions, capable of both good and bad, but he was smart enough to recognize opportunity when it came his way. He did not hesitate or second-guess himself. He acted with a confidence born deep in his soul. It was almost as if angels whispered to him on his way to earth: You will have wings—go and soar through the sky like an eagle.

At the end of his career, when American Airlines grounded him because of his health, Hank spent his time enjoying the company of women, speedboats, and his dogs, but there was emptiness there. When Hank called and asked his son to ride with him to Georgia that summer of 1968, Tift was glad to go along. Finally, Tift

thought that they might actually get to know one another. He knew that his father was depressed because he could no longer fly a plane and a trip to Georgia just might give him a lift. Even though it was brief, Tift was grateful for the time they had together.

Henry Tift Myers rests at the family plot at Oak Ridge Cemetery in Tifton. These words were carved upon his gravestone, written, more than likely, by Marguerite.

Master of His Profession

Capt. for American Airlines 35 years

Pilot for World Leaders in 1940's

Pilot of Presidents, Kings and Common Folk Too

Personal Pilot for President Franklin D. Roosevelt

and

President Harry S. Truman

In the days and weeks after his father's death, Tift received telegrams and letters from President Truman and President Lyndon Johnson. Cards were sent to him from around the nation and world expressing sympathy. Most of the major newspapers in the nation ran a picture and a story about the death of the first presidential pilot and aviation pioneer. Paul Harvey paid homage on his radio program. "Dad would be humbled and a bit embarrassed with all of the attention but it was certainly a wonderful

Henry Tift Myers, Sr. Circa 1950.

Tift's granddaughter Kaytlin believes that he can fix the moon! Photo by Bob Lukeman, Fort Worth.

Hotel Myon today—the home of City Hall. Photo by the author.

tribute to him and I felt a tremendous amount of gratitude," Tift said.

The Hotel Myon, lovingly operated by Irvine and Pearl Myers and home to Henry and Marguerite when they were young, is now home to the City of Tifton offices. The other Myers properties have long been sold. The new Henry Tift Myers airport was dedicated on March 15, 2003, and Tift was invited to say a few remarks about his father. Standing there at the beautiful new facility, he thought how very pleased his grandparents would be and how honored his dad would feel.

No, Hank Myers was not a traditional father and Tift might have missed out on receiving guidance and paternal influence. Every time, though, that Tift looks up and sees the moon, he recalls tender, magical memories when he was a small child and his dad would hold him tight and tell him that he was going to fix the moon the next time he went up in the sky. Now Tift's young granddaughters think that somehow he fixed the moon for them. A tradition begun more than fifty years ago has been passed down to another generation.

Today, when people hear Tift's name, there is usually a faint detection of something familiar and this same question always follows: "Was Lt. Col. Henry Tift Myers your father?" With the same charming smile his father had, Tift answers, "YES" with the deepest sense of pride. He is elevated and sent just about over the moon.

Epilogue

In 2003, Henry Tift Myers was nominated to be included in the Georgia Aviation Hall of Fame by virtue of the following accomplishments:

- First Presidential pilot

- Transport speed record, U.S. transcontinental for ten years

- First non-stop New York-Paris after Lindberg

- First non-stop London-Washington, D.C.

- First non-stop Hawaii-Alaska

- First non-stop Ceylon-Australia

- First around the world at the equator

- First U.S. aircraft into the Ascension Islands

- First Cairo-Bermuda-Washington D.C. via Azores

- First U.S. aircraft into Azores

- Distinguished Flying Cross for pioneering flights

- Air Medal with five Oak Leaf Clusters

- Commendation from General MacArthur for special flight for Senate Investigating Committee

- American Theatre Ribbon

- WWII Victory Ribbon

- American European-African Middle Eastern Ribbons

- Five Bronze stars for Asiatic Pacific Ribbon for campaigns New Guinea, India, Burma, China, Aleutian Islands, and Western Pacific

- Philippine Liberation Ribbon

- Commendation by Maj. Gen. Harold L. George for superior and skillful manner of handling transportation of the President of the United States and members of his staff to and from the Argonaut

Tift accepts for his father *The Wall of Fame* Award for Military Service.

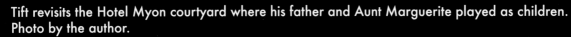

Tift revisits the Hotel Myon courtyard where his father and Aunt Marguerite played as children.
Photo by the author.

Conference in the Crimea (Argonaut was the code name for Yalta)

• Commendation by Mrs. Eleanor Roosevelt for efficiency and courtesy extended to her on trips to the Caribbean, South Atlantic, and Pacific

• Commendation by Henry L. Stimson, Secretary of War, for alert and capable manner displayed on trips to the Mediterranean and European Theaters

• Commendation by J.O. Richardson, Admiral, USN, for splendid cooperation rendered in connection with trip of Joint Chiefs of Staff to European and Mediterranean Theaters and to the Pacific and Southwest Pacific Ocean Areas

As of the printing of this book, Tift has not heard from the Georgia Aviation Hall of Fame committee but remains hopeful that in time, his father will indeed be inducted.

Lieutenant Colonel Myers was among those selected in 2003 for the Wall of Fame honoring Tift County natives who served in the military with distinction. Tift had the privilege of accepting the commendation for his father.

In honor of his grandparents' many contributions as pioneer citizens and business leaders of Tifton, Tift had the pleasure of presenting their portraits to the City of Tifton. Suitably, the likeness of Irvine and Pearl Myers grace the dining room wall of the Hotel Myon where they spent many happy years together. Now this same location is the home of City Council Chambers.

Tift has spoken with representatives from the Richard B. Russell Library for Political Research and Studies in Athens, Georgia, and is considering donating his father's documents, pictures and flight logs to the library for research. Lieutenant Colonel Myers and Senator Russell shared the home state of Georgia and both were graduates of the University of Georgia. The two men were good friends and literally traveled around the world together, so the Richard B. Russell Library may be the appropriate place to display the vast collection from Lieutenant Colonel Myers' career.

Speaking about his father has become a favorite past-time and Tift is honored when asked. If you know of a group that would enjoy hearing about the first presidential pilot, Tift may be reached at the following address:

Henry Tift Myers, Jr.

406 West 12th Street

Tifton, GA 31794

Phone: (229) 382-8780

Tift's diabetes and high blood pressure are under control and the move to Georgia has been positive. He loves the slower and simpler life of a small community. As it turned out, Pearl's cabin on the Alapaha River, built many years ago as a fish camp, was sold to his dearest friend's family and he has been given permission and a key to go and stay whenever he desires. In the pristine surroundings, while listening to the sounds of nature, he finds his connection to God and to his family. All is well. He has asked that after he dies, his ashes be spread along the river, where he finds wonderful peace.

Marguerite's delicate and wonderful cheese biscuits that were mentioned a couple of times in this book still have a loyal following, thanks to Doll Graydon. Doll came to work for Pearl Myers in 1948 and was her dear friend and employee until Pearl died in 1965. Doll and Marguerite were a team until Marguerite's death in 1996 and in Doll's words," I was one of a few people who could get along with Marguerite on a daily basis—we would get mad at each other but we always respected each other." Doll helped Marguerite make millions of the cheese biscuits and then delivered them to special friends that Marguerite thought worthy of receiving them. When this author tried to make the dainty biscuits, they turned out rather pitiful, a complete disaster and were quickly tossed out. Doll (who lives up to her name) was gracious enough to come over and show me the trick that makes the little daisy shaped delights almost as good as Marguerite's. I have included the recipe for those who may wish to try them. (Thank you, Doll, for keeping up the tradition.)

Tift speaking about his father at the dedication ceremony for the new Tifton airport. *The Tifton Gazette*, March 15, 2003.

1 pound extra sharp Kraft cheese (leave out overnight)
1 pound Land O' Lakes Margarine
2 tsp salt
Dash of cayenne pepper
Pillsbury All Purpose Flour (up to six cups)

Preheat over to 350 degrees.

Grate the cheese and then beat in an electric mixer, adding the margarine a quarter at a time. Continue to beat mixture until it is very light and fluffy (this takes a while—a good while, and when you think that you are done, keep on beating—that 's the trick; it is a labor of love.) Slowly add the flour, a half-cup at a time and then the salt and cayenne pepper. Continue beating the mixture until well-incorporated and very light to the touch.

Put the dough in a cookie press (daisy shape tip) and then onto a cookie sheet on the center rack of the oven. Watch closely and after 5 minutes or so turn the cookie sheet and continue cooking for another 4 or 5 minutes. You do not want them to turn brown – just until the tips change color. Remove to cake racks for cooling. Put in airtight containers and keep in a cool place—or freeze for up to one year.

Marguerite's cheese biscuits

A wonderful bit of synchronicity happened just as I finished writing this book. While my son and I were watching a video of old Red Skelton TV shows from the 1950s, there was Hank. Red came onto the stage and opened a telegram and said: "This is from Hank Myers and he says that I can take all the baggage I want to on his plane when he takes me to Miami to open at the Fontainebleau Hotel." (He said this as beautiful girls in bathing suits paraded by.) My son and I just looked at each other and were amazed at the wonderful coincidence. Again I had the feeling that Hank, from another dimension, was giving me the OK to write his story. It has been a wonderful experience learning a bit of history and getting to know the Myers family and their friends.

Thank each of you for spending some time with this book. If this story called to mind memories that you may have had of Hank or his family, we would love to hear from you. Your comments or questions are most welcomed.

Bonne Cella

1006 College Avenue North

Tifton, GA 31794

"A people without the knowledge of their past history, origin and culture is like a tree without roots."

Marcus Garvey

Fixing the Moon –the ballad
Written and Recorded by Davy Davis

I stood along the runway, and waved a faint goodbye
The taillights blinked in the darkness, as the plane began to fly,
Daddy had to leave again but he'd said he be home soon,
I know where he is tonight; he's gone to fix the moon,
He's gone to fix the moon

Little boys have lots of toys like trains & planes & trucks,
All the toys don't help a lot when you miss your dad so much,
Daddy had to leave again but he said he'd be home soon,
I know where he is tonight; he's gone to fix the moon,
He's gone to fix the moon

Fixing the moon, fixing the moon,
He'll be home soon, 'cause he's fixing the moon

Every night when I see the moon, I think of him and smile,
And wonder if he thinks of me as he logs away the miles,
Daddy had to leave again but he said he'd be home soon,
I know where he is tonight; he's gone to fix the moon,
He's gone to fix the moon

Tift holds 3 year-old Dow Johnston of Tifton, in a pose reminiscent of days gone by. Photo by the author.